THE LEGION
OF
THE DAMNED

THE LEGION OF THE DAMNED

The Adventures of
BENNETT J. DOTY
in the French Foreign Legion as Told by Himself

WESTHOLME
Yardley

Originally published in 1928 by The Century Company.

Westholme Publishing, LLC
904 Edgewood Road
Yardley, Pennsylvania 19067
Visit our Web site at www.westholmepublishing.com

ISBN: 978-1-59416-339-5
Also available as an eBook.

Printed in the United States of America.

TO

MY MOTHER

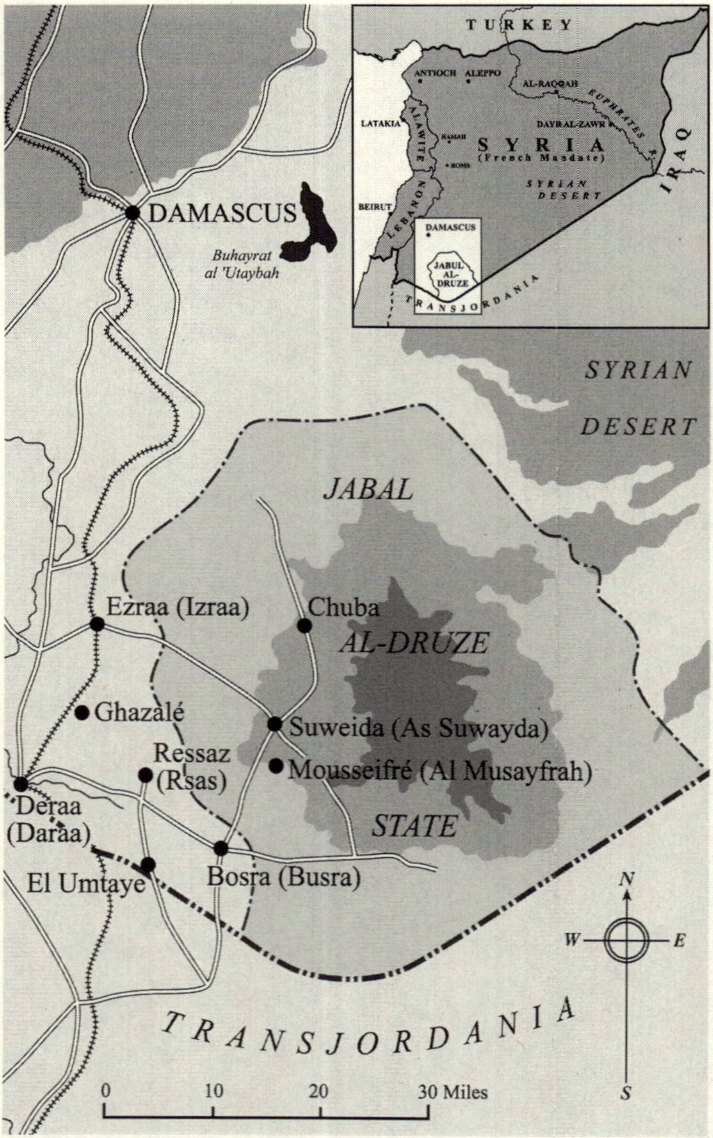

FRENCH MANDATE SYRIA IN 1925.

FOREWORD

I HAVE been asked by friends to write the account of my experiences while serving as a fighting private in the French Foreign Legion, and of the special ordeal I went through. These experiences form a rather extraordinary adventure, taking in a year's fighting in Syria, and culminating on June 6, 1926, when my father and mother, in their home in Tennessee, abruptly were faced with the news that, thousands of miles away and among strangers, I was about to be shot.

I say "culminating." Happily this was a culmination that was not an ending. I was not shot. And I am now back home once more, "libéré"—free!

I am sitting at a table in my room in our old house in the home town. Although the day is near Christmas, the window is open, for this is down in Mississippi. I can hear a tree rustling, there, just below the sill.

And I feel as though in a dream; or just having finished a dream—I don't know which.

It is hard to believe that I am really free. Every moment I expect to wake up. And find myself facing again the dread *Conseil de Guerre*, or within the narrow confines of my cell at Clairvaux Prison, or stretched in my little bunk at Sidi Bel Abbes. Events have happened so rapidly of late I can hardly believe that anything is real.

On December 1—just three weeks ago, I was with my regiment in Algeria, just reprieved from a terrible sentence. The regiment was getting ready to entrain for Morocco; I had before me a prospect of several more years of cruelly hard service away from country, friends and home. And suddenly on that day, December 1, I am notified that I am released from the Legion. Freed! I am to embark immediately for France.

Then follows the crossing of the Mediterranean on the French transport *Tafna*. We were in a great storm. My "bunk" consisted of just one fifth of the dining-room table of the small steamer. The other four fifths of the table belonged to four companions, four other Legionaires, discharged at the end of their long terms of enlistment. They averaged, I think, fatter than I was, for from my place on the western edge of the table every now and then I would find myself completely shoved off. And whenever an extra-big roll came along, off we would all slide, like a pile of slippery dishes off a tray. We were of five distinct nationalities; every time this happened, all in a heap on the tossing floor, we swore in five languages. And we were all seasick—what a crossing! And yet how happy I was!

I landed at Marseilles looking like a scarecrow. I had been terribly sick for two days and nights, I was unshaven, my hair was cropped close, as is the style in the Legion; I had slept in my clothes. And those clothes were the hand-me-downs the Legion presents to the discharged soldier as the last token of its affection and esteem. My sleeves stopped a little way below the elbow, my shoulders cracked everywhere through the cloth. They had been liberal though with the pantaloons. They were pants made for some giant; I could have gone entire into either one of the legs. No necktie, no collar, an undershirt without shirt—I was a sight.

Well, I shaved, I bathed. I couldn't do anything about my hair, which remained cropped close, but I did buy some clothes. They were French clothes—Marseilles clothes, to be exact—I did not look quite like the last pattern of a college boy of Harvard or Yale, but believe me, just to feel the soft cloth on me after those years of khaki, and the freshness of linen, that was a part of the dream I had walked into. And in another day I was strolling Monte Cristo's home town like the veriest tourist; and then the train, the luxurious Orient Express, with sleeping car, dining car, observation café; and then Paris.

Six days in Paris!

At Cherbourg I embarked on the *Majestic*, to return to my home, to the parents I had not seen for three and a half years and whom unwittingly I had placed on the worst of racks of uncertainty, fear and dread.

And let me tell you something which has to do, I think, with that relativity of Mr. Einstein's.

The *Majestic* is at present the largest liner afloat, a ship of fifty-six thousand tons, fitted with all the conveniences and luxuries known to man.

Well, the passage was rough. Gale upon gale hit us; we bucked a continuous head sea. But really it was not much worse than if you were in the Woolworth Building and it rocked a little. Yet on the third day I caught myself complaining at the length of the trip and the state of the sea.

I, only a few days ago Gilbert Clare, private of the French Foreign Legion, and barely escaped from a most unpleasant fate!

"Snap out of it, Gilbert Clare!" I said to myself. "Snap out of it!" I think this is going to be my motto from this day on.

And now as to this book which I am going to write—a new adventure on which I embark rather cheerfully, because I know I have something to say, and any one who really has something to say cannot go far wrong in the saying of it.

It was on June 12, 1925, that I enlisted in the Legion. All of the dramatic experiences that have befallen me since that day will be told with absolute truth and fidelity in this book. They will be told with no reservations, no pinkish glossings-over, but also without exaggeration. I wish the book to be a true human document.

Of the interest there is in the material itself, I think there can be no doubt.

For an entire year I was in the Foreign Legion, during some of the most desperate fighting that famous corps has ever done. And this in a far country, one of color and mystery and romance.

I had hardly completed my preliminary training in Algeria when I was assigned to the now famed Vingt-neuvième Compagnie de Marche, the Legion, hurled into Syria in August 1925, with revolt, fire and rapine reigning everywhere and the French sorely pressed.

In Syria we took part in all the most difficult and dangerous combats, including the battles of Mousseifré and Rezzas.

For its valor and devotion in these combats, and its faithful endurance in the terrific toil and murderous marching which went with them, the Vingt-neuvième Compagnie de Marche was given the fourragère.

This consists in the right of every man in the command to wear slung across his left shoulder a looped cord braided of scarlet and horizon blue. This distinction is accorded only for extraordinary service; the French Government gave it to some of our best troops during the big war. But in our case still another distinction was made. The right to the fourragère usually remains with the unit to which it is given; a soldier leaving such a unit cannot take the fourragère with him. Well, we were given that right. And now any soldier of the Vingt-neuvième, even if transferred, keeps his fourragère, and proudly wears it among the men of the less distinguished unit.

This for the company as a whole. As for myself personally, I received the croix de guerre.

Before going on, however, I feel obliged to correct a version of my adventures which has been widely spread and heralded in this country.

On June sixth, my father, in his home town in Tennessee, was notified by a representative of the press, that I, a soldier of the Foreign Legion in Syria, thousands of miles away, had been court-martialed, sentenced to death, and was about to be shot.

This, it proved later, was not quite true. Though, I must admit, disquietingly near it. I have never been sentenced to be shot.

For deserting I was sentenced to eight years in prison. Any one knowing about French prisons will be satisfied that this is enough to furnish a story, without the necessity of having me shot. I got eight years, just as did John Harvey, the Englishman who was one of my three companions in the rather unfortunate venture, and who in turn has just been released.

I shall not attempt to justify my desertion. I shall tell about it truthfully, with all the facts, what turmoil of the spirit made me do it, how we did it, how we failed.

And I was not charged with desertion in the face of the enemy. If I had I would have been shot, sure enough! At the time I "made my promenade," "took my little stroll," as the Legionaires say, the fighting in Syria was over. The French Foreign Legion, as were their Roman forebears, are great road-builders. We had been put to the construction of roads, of forts, of citadels—a heavy, grinding, gray, monotonous work—and how they do work you in the French Legion! No fighting, no excitement, no nothing. We had what the Legion calls "le cafard," a mixture of half-insanity from sheer monotony, and of nostalgia and homesickness. We were fed up, *and* fed up.

That is how we deserted.

I shall tell of the Foreign Legion as it is, and let the facts speak for themselves. I shall describe my training, my year of constant fighting, my desertion, capture and trial, and my eight long, weary, terrible months in five French prisons.

Out of these I was released through the tireless efforts of my father and of friends both in the United States and in France, of the American

Embassy in Paris, working upon the courtesy of the French Government and the clemency of the French Minister of War, Monsieur Painlevé. And, as Colonel Rollet, commander of my regiment, said to me upon my release, "Gilbert Clare, vous avez de la chance." I feel that on the whole I have been a lucky boy.

ILLUSTRATIONS

THE LEGION OF THE DAMNED

THE LEGION OF THE DAMNED

CHAPTER I

Why did I join the Legion? I have been asked that question many times. And usually I say, "I don't know." As a matter of fact I don't quite know. Who is sure of all the elements of the internal turmoil which sling a man into an abrupt decision? It was very suddenly I made up my mind to join that legendary fighting corps.

But Fate somehow had already spoken. For instance, I was born on a plantation in Alabama, near the town of Demopolis. Many of the inhabitants of that region are descendants of French Huguenots, driven away from France by religious persecution far back in the days of the great Cardinal Richelieu.

Then, back in the middle of the last century, my great-grandfather, a Southern lawyer, defended in New Orleans a luckless Frenchman who had been accused of murder. So well did he acquit himself that the man was freed, and that under orders of Louis Philippe, the King of France, the great minister and historian Guizot sent to my father an autographed letter of thanks which we still have in the family. In the family we also have a table made by the Frenchman who had been in peril. He fashioned it in token of gratitude for my grandfather, out of all the woods that grow in the South, and that table is now in the living room of our home in Biloxi, Mississippi.

Then came the World War, which took me to France. For my soldiering in the Foreign Legion was not my first soldiering.

In April 1917, we were living in Memphis, my father, my mother, my brother and I. I was then a high school lad, sixteen years old. I went down to the Armory, executed on paper a little hocus-pocus about my age, and enlisted in the First Tennessee Regiment of the National Guard. This later became the 55th Artillery Brigade, in the Thirtieth Division. And with this unit, an artilleryman shooting the big 155 shorts, I went through the big fracas of St. Mihiel and the Argonne.

Mustered out and back home again in April 1919, I started to take up the old thread again. But it was not so good. It was too smooth and straight a thread after all that excitement. I attended Vanderbilt University one year, then the University of Virginia for almost three. I studied literature and economics. I played a little football. I went to dances. When the year 1923 started, I decided on a fresh start. I left the university and went to work.

But that did not seem to be so good either. It was office work. It was picayunish, monotonous work, it kept me inside. I stuck it out a year. Then, not knowing just what I was doing with myself, I went off on an automobile trip with a friend, John Turk. We toured Kentucky, we went up north. We landed in New York.

And then I went to sea. And that was the last my parents were to hear of me till two years later they received the word that I was about to be shot in Syria. I stopped writing. I didn't feel I had much to write which would give them any pleasure. I wasn't at all certain they would answer such letters.

For a year I hit the sea, first as deck boy, then as ordinary seaman, on coast schooners, Shipping

Board vessels, United States Fruit liners. I went to South America, I went to Europe.

In April 1925, I was on a fruit boat in New Orleans when I began to read in the paper of the fighting in Morocco. Abd-el-Krim had broken loose and was raising Cain. There seemed to be a lot of color and excitement about existence over there. I was rather fed up with life upon the bounding wave as seen by an ordinary seaman from the deck of a modern steamer. That color, that excitement, that smell of powder over there began to intrigue me. I stayed on the ship till we had reached New York. Immediately I found a boat leaving for Bordeaux. They needed no seamen; I shipped as mess steward. I was bound to get to Bordeaux somehow or other. For I had decided to join the Legion.

On the boat, the wireless kept us in touch with the turmoil of the fighting over there. Abd-el-Krim was sweeping forward everywhere. And the sailors talked of the fighting and of the Legion and of friends they had in that grim band.

I was being led along by no childish illusions. The books I had read about the Legion were rather black ones. But I thought, "In those there

is as much apple-sauce as in the giddy romantic Ouida ones. The truth is somewhere in between, and I'll soon be finding it out."

Among the mess stewards was a young French boy, who seemed to take it as his duty to cure me before it was too late. He'd stand and look at me, shaking his head. "So you are going into that *enfer?*" he would say.

"O la, la!" He'd snap his finger. "O la, la! But you'll be a sorry one! *Mon vieux*, my old one, wait till you've been there an hour. O la, la, but you'll be calling for your mother!"

The boy meant well. Although he exaggerated, looking back now I sometimes think that as a mentor and counselor, he was not so bad.

We arrived in Bordeaux June 11, 1925, and it was not long before I was looking for the Bureau des Engagements Volontaires. I found it—a tiny little office tucked away in a corner of the big building of the Military Headquarters. Behind a desk sat a mild-looking middle-aged officer. When he got up, he walked about leaning heavily on a stick—a cripple, evidently, of many campaigns. He greeted me courteously; he was fatherly and benign; he asked me what I wanted.

"Can I engage here for the Légion Etrangère?" I asked.

"Mais oui, monsieur." He was all politeness and acquiescence. "Pray, be seated."

Seated there, I gave him the many particulars he demanded. Name, parentage, nationality. When he asked me my name, I was stuck only for an instant. I gave the first name that popped into my head. And that was Gilbert Clare.

How was it this name had popped into my head? Queerly enough. Some years before I had been reading a history of the Norman conquest of England. The Clares appeared in this history—a Norman family that had settled in Ireland at the time of William the Conqueror, and were hardy soldiers. The name had evidently caught my fancy. "Gilbert Clare"—out it now popped.

It has been my name now for two years. It has sometimes been spoken sweetly to me, but mostly it has been resoundingly bawled. And it became so much a part of me that even now, there are moments when I ask myself, "Are you Bennett Doty, or are you Gilbert Clare?" And anywhere, were some one to shout behind me, "Gilbert Clare!" I surely would jump in the air and turn with my hands along the seams of my trousers, at attention.

"You will return to-morrow for the necessary physical examinations," said the officer. And then, "Bonjour, monsieur."

And I went out to stroll the last hours of freedom I was to have for a good long while.

I took the physical examinations the next day. The Legion may not be very careful of the moral character of its candidates, but it is extremely fussy on the physical side. I was made to hop about on one foot till I almost dropped. I made my own world's record in the deep bend. I touched the floor with my hands till I had worn a distinct depression in the wood. All my joints were rotated like windmills to test their flexibility. And I passed A1.

Then I signed and was given an order for train fare to Port-Vendres, a small seaport on the Spanish frontier. I was now a Legionaire.

Early the next morning, I dropped from the train at Port-Vendres, and walked over to the barracks of the *Tirailleurs Senegalais*, whom I will describe only by saying that they were the exact reverse of lily-white. I remained there several days, well fed and lodged. Then of a morning, with a nondescript crowd of zouaves, tirailleurs and Chasseurs d'Afrique, I embarked on the *Mustapha II* for Oran, in Algeria. With me were only two recruits for the Legion, and both were Spaniards. One of them had fought in Morocco with the Queen's regiment. The other men —zouaves, tirailleurs, chasseurs—were men on leave rejoining their commands, and right there I got my first impression of the color of the East, what with their uniforms in which appeared hues as gay as scarlets and tender as azure blues. We arrived at Oran the next afternoon, and a corporal was there to escort the two Spaniards and me to the Petit Dépôt of the Legion.

He was a young Russian, blond, blue-eyed, snappy and good-looking. He wore the khaki uniform which the Legion uses in campaigning, and it was bleached from much washing. Across his chest were all his campaign ribbons; he combined absolute neatness with a commanding bearing, and the sight of him somehow raised my heart which had begun to drop a little.

"You are for the Legion?" he asked.

"Yes."

"Follow me," he ordered.

We followed him up a steep bluff, and up there entered the city. He walked briskly ahead, eyes fixed, looking neither to the right nor the left, all at his duty, unconscious of the welter of life and color through which we plowed. And we three recruits followed, all eyes, twisting our necks, stumbling now and then what with trying to hold his stiff pace, with our eyes not at all on the pavement, but on the swirling colored costumes, the swarming shops and cafés. Then we were outside the city again, and going along a long lane, and before us, behind high white walls, rose the barracks of the spahis, zouaves and tirailleurs, buildings which knocked my eyes out what with their size, their cleanliness and beauty. One of the gates was guarded by a soldier with an enormous mustache. We entered this one. We were at the Dépôt of the Legion.

Our mentor took us to the guard room where I presented my papers to the sergeant in charge, a little square-shouldered Frenchman with a ferocious mustache which rose on each side of his nose. He passed his eyes over my papers, mumbling to himself. He came to the line giving the nationality. "*Tiens*," he said, "you are American? Well, there's another one here; you're going to have a *camarade*."

"Call Phillips," he ordered.

I heard the bawled name go echoing all through the barracks, "Phee-leeepe, Phee-leeepe!" while I waited, wondering who might be the countryman and comrade Fate was bringing me. And suddenly, ahead of the bawling voice, down the stairs came eagerly tumbling a big black boy. "Voilà Phillipe," said the sergeant proudly.

Well, Phillips was black all right—about as black as they make them; in America, at least—but he proved a true friend during those first confusing and a bit discouraging days. "White folks!" he exclaimed, and stood stock-still. Then, "Has you joined up? Come along an' I'll fix you up."

He took me up to the sleeping quarters and picked out a bunk for me, considering long and judiciously, and for the next few days he appointed himself my guardian. He saw that I got enough to eat, he was my official interpreter, as I then spoke but little French, picking it up as I went along. He saved me from a great business blunder. Many of my new fellow soldiers wanted to buy my civilian clothes, now useless to me. It seemed that such were a matter of important trafficking at the Petit Dépôt of the Legion in Oran. I was ready to take one of the first offers when he stopped me. "Don't yuh sell 'em heah, don't yuh sell 'em heah," he warned me. "You can git moah for dem at the Big Depot, at Bel Abbes." And this I found true when I got to Sidi Bel Abbes—not an unimportant matter seeing that at the time my pay in the Legion was just exactly three francs seventy-five centimes per fifteen days, with the franc worth about three cents at that.

He was not all rock of assurance, however. As we went about he had a way of stopping short and hitting his puzzled head. "Wot the devil are you doin' in this damned outfit!" he would exclaim, his eyes rolling. "Man, you is made a big mistake. Too late now."

"Me," he would say humbly, "dat don't matter. But you—what are you doing in this hell hole! Man, but you sure is made a big mistake. Too late, now!"

I never did learn much about Phillips, whose first name was Charles. Our ways parted soon after, when I went on to Sidi Bel Abbes. He hailed from California, I believe, and had then served four and a half years in the Legion, where he had achieved of late the position of railway station guard.

There are always some Americans in the Legion. Some of these I met a little later at the big depot of Sidi Bel Abbes. One of those I liked best was "Big" Nicholls of the Musique who played almost everything in the band. He was a long Texan, and introduced me to the canteen and my first bottle of wine. He was an old regular, who had served in the American cavalry and had been first sergeant. He seemed to know every one in the Legion, and I liked nothing better than to sit over a bottle of wine with him at the canteen, listening to his stories, as he sucked steadily at a villainous black pipe stoked with the strong Algerian tobacco. He had joined the Legion in 1920, and at the end of his first term of enlistment of five years, had engaged himself for another five. He is now in the Second Regiment, in Mekinez, in Morocco.

Then there was "Big Slim" Cheneyworth, who stood six feet six inches and was thin as a rail. He was a farmer boy from Iowa, who from his youth had handled mules, and his enlistment had not changed his profession; here also he was driving mules. His great trouble and the source of his constant anxiety was the getting of clothes big enough to cover his frame. With his six feet six he was here like a man from another race, dropped from another planet; none of the equipment fitted him. The company tailor sewed on extra strips to his sleeves so that he might cover his gaunt red wrists; additions had to be built on his slacks. And he had to curl up in his insufficient bunk when in barracks, and campaigning, his blanket was too short, so that in winter he was always cold.

Then there was Thompson, an ex-gob, who hailed from northern New York. He had already done his five years in the Legion and had signed on for five more. The last I heard of him he had gone out on a draft to the Fourth Regiment in Mekinez. Olsen, a *bleu*, a recruit, had been a dancer on the vaudeville stage.

There were many other Americans scattered throughout the Legion, but they were serving in other parts of the land, and I never ran across them and knew of them only by hearsay. Nicholls, Cheneyworth, Thompson and Olsen themselves I never saw again after my short stay at Sidi Bel

Abbes. No Americans were with me or near me after that; now and then rumor would bring me word of one or the other of them. Some vague news, where they were, in what outfit, what doing; and hearing thus about them made me feel a bit wistful—when there was time for it, which was seldom.

Of all these men I asked the question which now is so often asked of me in the States, "Why did you join the Legion?" Or, rather, "What made you join the Legion?"

And the answers would be the same—and a little bit like mine. They did not quite know, they could not clearly tell you. I found this to be almost always the case with men from other nationalities in the Legion. They were ready enough to talk of their lives till the narrative approached their enlistment; it then became befogged and vague, and finally ended in reticence and silence. Perhaps the reason for this is to be found in the following passage by the French writer, André Maurois:

> All civilizations have their sufferers. In every country in Europe, and without doubt in America also, live men for whom life is a penance. Some of them have been stricken down by misfortunes or by unforeseen happenings, and the sight of the places where they have

been unhappy has become unbearable for them. Others have suffered by their own mistakes or they have committed some act for which their consciences reprove them; they know that they can reconstruct themselves only by escaping from their pasts. For all those beings, for all those whom Dostoevski calls the "Insulted and the Injured," the Foreign Legion offers a refuge.

This may fit Europeans better than it fits us, and be a rather highfalutin explanation for the acts of American boys. But—well, anyway, I have now told how it was I joined the Legion. Or have I? Maybe.

You see there was down South a girl I liked. And she is now married . . . not to me.

CHAPTER II

THE Petit Dépôt at Oran is a sort of clearing house for the Legionaires. There they arrive, from there they depart after enlistment or discharge. And the men on leave, the *permissionnaires*, pass through here on their way to France, and return here, their leave over. The dépôt is a beautiful little building, of Moorish style, with verandas and balconies, and is spotlessly clean. Here indeed I made my first acquaintance with the absolute cleanliness of the French Foreign Legion.

Twice a day the floor and staircases, which are of tile, were washed and scrubbed; how many times a day they were swept, Heaven only knows. The *carré du quartier* was meticulously policed; not a scrap of paper, not a cigarette butt, not a toothpick ever was to be seen there. My first days in the Legion made me wonder whether I had not made a mistake, and turned myself into a scrubwoman, instead of a trooper in a crack corps. I washed tiles, I scrubbed them, I polished them.

I swept, I swabbed. I paced the *quartier*, a hood on my back, stooping twenty times at each step to pick up infinitesimal bits of matter out of place. And there was also the kitchen police; there are no servants in the Legion. I peeled potatoes and cut up carrots and shelled peas.

It was to be thus during my entire stay in the Legion. I never saw barracks, a post, a camp, which was not scrupulously clean and inspected twice a day. Woe to the man with dust under his bed, or dirty clothes in his pack. His number was up. He was due for four days of extra duty the first time; eight days in the *boîte*, the "box," the prison, the second time; and a regular course of progressive chastisement if he held to his slothful way. Cleanliness is the Legion's only claim to kinship with godliness; realizing this, they make the most of it.

At Oran, my hair was all clipped off (cleanliness again!). I was ordered (I was willing) to scrub under a hot shower bath. All men going to Sidi Bel Abbes, the headquarters of the Legion in Algeria, must arrive shaved, bathed and shorn.

After a few days in Oran, I left for Sidi Bel Abbes—or Bel Abbes, as the Legionaires familiarly dub it, together with fifty or sixty recruits of all nations, complexions and tongues. The train wound inland, only eighty kilometers, but at freight-train speed, a wearisome journey, and it was nearly dark when we arrived. We were formed by threes; in the dusk we marched along the outside of great walls, a bit like malefactors—evidently no one was proud of us. Suddenly we debouched into a large street which ran straight through the middle of town.

This was the main street of Sidi Bel Abbes, and the barracks of the Legion ran along each side. We passed the sentinel who stood on guard with bayonet fixed to his Lebel, and the strap of his kepi cutting his chin—and we were inside.

Over to our *caserne* we were marched, and up three flights of stairs to the *chambres* of the *bleus*, or recruits. In each chamber were twenty-eight little iron beds, and on every bed a complete change of uniform. Each of us, under order, stood at the head of his bed, dropped the clothing in which he stood and put on instead the outfit waiting on the bed. These were temporary uniforms; no attempt had been made to suit the wearer, and we emerged from this looking like a circus. My trousers were too long and my coat was too short; about me was every kind of misfit. We then received a cup of black coffee, meat and bread; shortly afterward, taps sounded, and we gladly went to bed.

There was just a little green light at the windows, when at five-thirty the sharp notes of the bugle woke me up, and almost immediately a corporal was bawling "Allez! Debout! Allez! Debout!" He was an easy-going corporal. After this I usually found that the corporals started shouting "Allez! Debout!" quite some time before the bugle, instead of with it.

Wearily we rolled out; each of us had a cup of very black coffee with a pinch of sugar, and then the corporal showed us how to make our beds.

This is quite a meticulous proceeding, almost a ceremony in the Legion. The blankets are folded into perfect squares and laid at the foot of the bed. The sheets are rolled into two cylinders, one of which is laid across the right extremity of the blanket square, the other across the left. The pillow is placed between them, in the exact center. After the beds had been made, each man swept up the floor under his bed and within his area, and then washed it carefully with a wet rag.

A whistle shrilled. "Au rassemblement!" the

corporal cried, and we dashed madly down the stairs for roll-call. Here I first met with the sergeant of the Legion in his full majesty and power.

For the sergeants of the Legion are not mild individuals of limited authority. Their prestige, their power, make of them nearly commissioned officers. They wear gold stripes, they live apart from hoi polloi, with their own mess, their own cooks, barmen, waiters and staffs. Each has his orderly; everything is done to give them prestige.

And they do command. They are the cement and the rock of the Legion, devoted, tireless, bearing the brunt of the training and the fighting. They glory in their work, they are priests of the traditions of the Legion, they are the mainstay of the regiments.

They are rough, of course, most of them. They roar a good deal. They are martinets as to discipline, bitterly critical judges of the niceties of the manual of arms. They are of all nationalities, and in character, some are good and some are bad. But in all my stay I never witnessed any real brutality, nor any sergeant of the type of Lejaune in "Beau Geste." As a matter of fact that would be impossible in the Legion. A brutal sergeant would not live long in a hard-boiled outfit like the Legion. He'd be murdered in his sleep. I did know some, however, who seemed to inflict punishment upon their men for the sheer joy of it.

I shall always remember my first sight of a sergeant. "Garde à vous!" our corporal cried as he appeared, springing rigidly to attention. Every one with a start immediately stiffened into an exact imitation of the corporal, and my lord came in. I thought of course he was a commissioned officer, what with his fine uniform, a colonel at least and maybe a general. He asked a few questions, then left the room, and we relaxed.

I turned to my neighbor, who spoke a little English. "Who was he?" I asked, in awe.

"A sergeant," he said.

On the same day we went before the *médecin major* for final examinations. These were extremely severe, still more severe than the one I had already undergone in Bordeaux. We bent, we twisted, we hopped, we rotated our joints, while our lungs, our hearts were being listened to. It takes more than a weakling to make the grade in the Legion, which is always at work. Terrific marches, guard duty in rain, wind and bitter cold are only the least of the hardships of a Legionaire.

The Legion is a great road-builder and civilizer; in it one lays down the rifle only to take up the ax, the pick, the spade, or the trowel. When the Legion marches it shakes a mean foot, and it marches with a wicked load on its back. It is always the chosen body, whether it is extraordinary valor or élan which is called for or simply mean hard labor and hardship. "*La légion, elle trappe toujours*—she always catches it, the Legion." I may add, "she" is always there.

We were more than seventy men taking the test. We were in our underwear, most of us were nervous. Every time our voices rose a little too loudly, out dashed a corporal, and rudely shut us up, threatening us with prison if we did not shut up. We shut up quickly enough; already we had learned of the power a mere "cabo" wields in the Legion.

"Clare!" they finally called, and recognizing my assumed *nom de guerre* to which already I was getting accustomed, in I dashed. When I had gone through the strenuous performance, and finally stood still, panting, the doctor said, "So, you are an American."

"Oui, mon capitaine," I replied.

"I served near the Yankees during the war," he

said, "and I knew many officers of your fine army. You are in excellent physical condition; try to remain so, and beware of the *pinard*. Good day and good luck."

The *pinard* is the red wine served in the canteens. Remembering the kind man's words, I bewared. Moderately.

We received the next morning the injection against typhus and typhoid (which made me sick for two days), then we who had passed were marched into a separate room where our sergeant addressed us. If in any of us remained any illusions as to a possibility of idle and romantic days, we lost the last trace of them then and there.

Said our sergeant, standing very straight before us, his gray eyes searching ours:

"You are now commencing your career in the Legion. Before you can see actual service, you must pass through four months or more of instruction, the time depending on your quickness to learn. During this period you will be called upon to endure many unaccustomed hardships and to bear the rough side of the instructor's tongue.

"But there is a little thing you must remember, which will serve to sober you whenever you begin to see red. I, the instructor, the corporals, the sergeants, the adjutants, the adjutant-generals, we have all been through the same mill. Remember that, and keep a stiff upper lip."

Here he stopped and grinned reminiscently.

"You will get your share of glory and hardship," he went on. "Our motto is *Honneur et Fidélité; Valeur et Discipline.*"

Then suddenly he made a little gesture. "Rompez!" he cried, and we broke ranks, dismissed.

We were sent to the *magasins* and each of us was given a completely new uniform—kepi, capote, khaki uniform, two suits of underwear, two shirts, and the *ceinture bleue*—a long strip of blue woolen cloth a foot wide and ten feet long, which, wrapped around the waist, is the distinctive mark of the Legionaire. We received a pair of *brodequins*, the marching shoe of leather thick as elephant hide, and thick-soled with several pounds of hobnails; we received a *bidon*—a water-bottle which holds two quarts—and finally our *musette*—the small sack for personal effects.

This time the equipment was being doled out with some regard as to the size and conformation of the wearer. I came out looking like a soldier.

CHAPTER III

AFTER we had been fully equipped we had our first inspection by our commander, Colonel Rollet.

It was a blinding hot day in June. Early in the morning we started to get ready under the bawlings of our sergeant. We were to be in parade dress—a compound of meticulous details in the Legion. We put on our uniforms. With the temperature near one hundred, we put on our heavy overcoats, our capotes, with the forward flaps turned back. And around these we wrapped our blue sashes. At review sashes are of account. Over that we slung our *bidon* and our *musette*, the first at a prescribed place to the right, the other to the left. In the *carré* full of the sun's blinding white glare, we were hauled this way and that by the sergeant, our costumes rectified, and after having been loudly called all species of animals, we finally managed to get ourselves lined up in single file to meet the colonel.

Followed a long wait, as we stood there in line, in the terrible heat, silently sweating and choking in our overcoats, our sashes and equipment. Then there was a sudden movement and bustle at the *poste de police*, we saw the guard lined up, presenting arms, our sergeant roared, "Garde à vous!" we snapped to attention, and Colonel Rollet came swinging down the line.

Colonel Rollet! I had heard much of him already, and now know still more. Grand Commander of the Legion of Honor, Colonel of the Premier Régiment, Etrangère, he is truly the Grand Old Man of the Legion, in which he has commanded (first as a young lieutenant) for nearly thirty years. During the World War, he commanded a battalion of the Legion's First *Régiment de Marche*, a body thrown into every one of that war's worst furnaces, and close to complete annihilation over and again. Covered with scars and decorations, but uniformed so simply that it is a standing joke with his men that he draws the same outfit as they do, he is never without the Legion's fourragère flung across his left shoulder.

He now came down the line, a little broad-shouldered man with a spade beard and fiercely turned-up mustache streaked with gray, and a nose like an eagle's beak. Before each man he stopped, sweeping him with a glance that took in every detail of his person and equipment, then asked him his name and nationality, and went on.

And finally he was before me, and I saw his eyes, his legendary, terrible blue eyes. They had passed rapidly over me, he had asked me my name and country, and I had answered, and now they were searching my own with that steady gaze of his, like that of an old falcon. I looked him right back in the eye. That is what he wanted. "Bien," he said shortly, and passed on to the next man. Each he searched thus, and to each steady look back, "Bien," he would say, and pass on.

When we had finished, feeling rather like school children now ready for a holiday, we were told that we were leaving that very afternoon for Saida, where the recruit is given the famous Legion training. We had heard already about that trip; it had been sardonically held out to us by the veterans. You ride all day in a train, then you disembark and march all night, a full twenty-eight kilometers, then you ride again the rest of the way; and this, when the men are still soft, with new and stiff equipment, is supposed to be an eloquent forerunner of what life in the Legion holds out for you.

So bitterly cursing at the news, cursing in sixteen tongues, we got ready for our hegira. After a hasty meal, we stormed down to the station in great style, heads up, arms swinging, behind the *Clique* with its fifes and drums, its bugles and trumpets, and those fast stirring tunes which, shrieked by the trumpets' high notes, catch a man by the spine. But that was the last of military splendor for the time. At the station the *Clique* about-faced and left us; in silence we crowded into the hot stuffy coaches, our heavy overcoats still on, and after a leisurely wait the train started creeping.

And thus it crept and crawled all afternoon, at that snail pace known only to an Algerian *omnibus* train. Little by little the heat increased, and crowded like cattle, we smothered in our capotes, which of course we had still on, regulations being regulations in the Legion. The train crawled and crawled, we almost died. Finally at about five, we reached a speck on the map with an unpronounceable name, and the sergeant roared, "Everybody out!"

Out we went gladly—only to discover there was to be no recess. Without a moment's loss of time we were lined up in a column by threes, "En avant," called the lieutenant in charge, and we were off along the white hard road for our twenty-eight-kilometer march.

The system—which is the one used in the French army—was to march for fifty minutes, then rest ten. For fifty minutes, you'd step along at a brisk pace, then you'd throw yourself on your back and hold your aching feet to the sky for ten minutes, then you'd step along some more. The men joked; they struck up marching songs; right here I was introduced to interesting refrains from all the armies of the world, which I am sorry to say I cannot quote, this book being one which is designed to be passable through the mails. For a time, everything went well. Then little by little the joking stopped, the singing ceased, the march passed through a dogged silence of endurance, and finally sighs, curses and groans began to be heard in the darkness of the ranks here and there.

As for me, my feet were swelling. I had on, as did all the other men, my newly issued *brodequins*. The French *brodequin*, even when old and well broken, is not vici-kid pump; new, its uppers seem to be fashioned of cast-iron. And the sole is thick and seemingly made of wood thickly coruscated with hobs. Each shoe, as I raised it in turn, seemed to be a whole keg of nails; and little by little, what was within it was becoming one large sore blister. As the hours passed, and we tramped, tramped, tramped, the sounds of distress increased. And finally when we staggered up to the small railway station which was our destination, we all simply wanted to lie down and die.

But we did not lie down and die. Off the sergeant sent us to collect wood. We built a fire. Soon we had a great kettle of coffee beginning to bubble. Rations were served out as the sun rose—bread and cheese, and that tinned meat which the French call "singe," which means monkey. We breakfasted, then with great pain took off our shoes. I held my big bare feet up in the air. I did not recognize them at all; they were not the old pedal comrades faithful to me so long; they were dissociated from me, the pain itself did not seem to belong to me, but to float about; they looked like hams—suffering hams.

After a good rest, I replaced them gingerly within the *brodequins*. The train had slid into the station and was waiting for us—freight cars, this time; our old friends of the *quarante hommes* and *huit chevaux*. In we piled. Three hours more of this, and we were in Saida, in which we were to pass many weary hours of training.

The ground had risen about us as we went. We were now in a rough and semi-mountainous country, affording good conditions for the training of the Legionaire fated to combat in Morocco and Syria.

We slept well that night—there was no insomnia. They did not rush us too much the next day, either. We were assigned to chambers, twenty-eight men in each chamber under a corporal dubbed "chef de chambre." We passed the day in peaceful housekeeping, arranging our chamber, and being put through a thorough course in the arrangement of the sacrosanct *paquetage.*

In the French Foreign Legion, the soldier makes his pack by folding all of his clothing into squares of precisely the same size, which are then laid one on top of the other in a manner exactly prescribed. A glorified sandwich it is, but one with no rough edges, you may believe, and nothing sticking out. To make the *paquetage* in the approved fashion requires much practice; let the slightest bit of it be out of line, or a little crooked along the roll, and blooey! the inspecting corporal or sergeant, with one sweep of the hand, destroys the painstakingly built cube and contemptuously scatters it over the floor. This is rather trying at times, but one must learn to hold one's temper in the Legion. A bad temper is a luxury that counts dearly in the Legion; I know men now serving five years in prison for losing their heads and striking or cursing a non-com who disapproved of their *paquetage!*

Early the next morning, we were aroused by the bugle, and the corporal was shouting, "Debout!" At six-thirty we were already out for drill without arms, as no arms are given until one has learned the facings. We marched to the drill field, and there we just naturally caught hell.

First came an hour of drill at double-quick time, mixed with a savage dose of setting-up exercises, something grimly known in the Legion as the Legion's breakfast. After this we had the different facings and the commencement of squad drill.

The really terrific drilling given in the Legion is one of its traditions. The movements are much the same as those used in other armies, but the Legion demands a precision in each gesture far beyond that asked elsewhere. The Legion sergeant, the Legion non-com is an inexorable fanatic on this subject. A movement must be done *comme il faut*, and his *comme il faut* is an ideal close to the limits of physical possibility. To gain his end, a sergeant of the Legion will make a man repeat a thousand times if necessary. The recruit will repeat till he is ready to murder, he will repeat till ready to drop with exhaustion, but under that sergeant's implacable eye and his crescendo roarings, he will repeat till he has learned to do the movement *comme il faut!*

At nine-thirty, having drilled steadily for three long hours, we reëntered the barracks for company assembly, at which the report was read, and then at ten o'clock, came *la soupe*. This was not misnamed; there was soup. And a piece of boiled meat and a vegetable. And with this we received a half loaf of bread and a *quart* of wine (about half a pint) for the day. And then *repos!*

This mid-day rest, the siesta, is peculiar to the Legion and to the clime, and is absolutely necessary in the hot months, when the mid-day sun makes of the courts, of the whole land, a furnace. The men are not allowed outside during this period; they are supposed to remain in the barracks and to sleep. At two-thirty, we were back at drill, and then steadily at it again till five, upon which the recall was sounded for the second *soupe*. After that one was free to go into town till nine, when came *l'appel*, the roll-call. Free, I mean, of course, unless it was your turn for guard duty, which came around often enough, and if you had the strength left to stagger out.

After a few days, the drills without arms became drill with arms. Gradually we adjusted our lives to our new environment, and settled down to the monotony of constant drill. Sunday was our day of rest. On Sundays we washed our clothes, ironed our linen and sewed on our buttons!

It was during this period that I came first to learn there was some truth in the stories abroad about the iron discipline of the Legion.

When, last December, I was leaving the Legion, I was called before my commander, Colonel Rollet.

"I know that you are going to write about the Legion," he said to me. "Well, write. But tell the truth. *Nous sommes durs*," he said, "*mais nous sommes justes*. We are hard, but we are just."

Going back over my experience in the Legion, it hits me that Colonel Rollet is right. Hard the Legion certainly is; cruelly hard I found the life there. But it is just.

The slightest misdemeanor was promptly punished, and without indulgence. A dirty rifle cost anywhere from four days to eight days in prison; dust under the bed, a dirty mess-kit, soiled clothes in the *paquetage*, any of these meant eight days of the "plute."

The "plute" is the time-honored punishment of the Legion. The men so to be punished are marched around the prison court, in step and regular formation for as much as nine hours a day, each bearing upon his back a thirty-kilogram sack of sand. To those curious of particulars, I may add that a kilogram is the equivalent of two and one tenth of our pounds, so that a thirty-kilo sack of sand is a seventy-pound sack of sand. To those still more curious I will own that I have carried around this little sack of sand. For eight days running. It is a sack designed to cool the hottest head—and for an unlucky moment I had been a hot-head.

Never in the Legion have I seen, and never have I heard of men being beaten, nor of being driven off into the desert, as has been shown in a recent popular film.

Discipline in the Legion is largely in the hands of the sergeants, and they take this part of their job—and all other parts—seriously. These *sous-*

officiers, these non-coms, are the backbone of the Legion. The sergeant knows his men. Their failings he knows, their foibles and their weaknesses; and also their qualities and their virtues. He is the lord of high, middle and low justice; he deals it out without hesitation, and with an unsparing hand.

While we were drilling there in Saida, news was drifting in, and rumor, that told us all was not well with the République. Morocco was in turmoil, and Abd-el-Krim playing the devil. At the other end of the Mediterranean, the Druses, fierce tribesmen who inhabit the mountains of Lebanon and the Grand Liban, of the Jebel Hauran and the Jebel Druse, had risen in revolt against their French administrators. Syria was aflame, an entire French column of four thousand men had been cut off and destroyed. And out of Saida daily, and out of Sidi Bel Abbes, drafts were going out to fill up the Legion's heavy losses.

I asked if I could go.

"You'll go when you are wanted, and not before," the sergeant answered.

Then with a grin—and it was rare for him to grin—he added, "But you'll be wanted, have no fear!"

And one fine day a long list was called out among which was my name; we of the list were going to Sidi Bel Abbes. In Bel Abbes we were placed in a *compagnie de passage*. Everything seemed in disorder in this "passing" company; men were continuously being called out for physical examinations, to receive back pay, discharge or leave. But one morning the sergeant in charge stood before us with a sheet of paper.

"The following men," he announced, "will form a company of march for Tunisie. They will report for a complete change of clothing and equipment."

Tunisie? We looked at each other and winked. Tunisie was a peaceful province living in profound peace. But from Tunisie went the boats which landed fresh forces in war-torn Syria.

He began to read the names on his list, and the third one was Gilbert Clare!

Thus was born the famous "Vingt-neuvième Compagnie du Premier Régiment de la Légion Etrangère"—a company which, though promising very little at the time, was to make one of the most wonderful records of any company in a regiment accustomed to wonderful records.

And I knew I was going to Syria.

CHAPTER IV

THE newly formed company of which I was now a part, the Vingt-neuvième Compagnie du Premier Régiment Etrangère, deserves a few words. It was a queer, loose and mixed lot at first. Looking it over no esthetic thrill grabbed your spine; you were apt to wonder whence came this remarkable assortment of villainous gentlemen. As a matter of fact they came from all parts of the world and from all walks of life—mainly, not very high ones. I think that no officer really expected much good from them. A spirit of sardonic humor seemed to have attended its formation.

The Premier Régiment, of which it was a part, was one which owned to a particular fame gained in the World War. It had been transported to France in 1914, recruited up till it numbered four thousand men and then thrown into the furnace. In its first action, charging in the face of machine gun fire, across trenches and barbed wire, it had been virtually annihilated. Recruited up to strength again, it had gone on thus through the entire war, depleted almost to nothing over and over again—a sort of sacrificial corps, ever at the worst place.

The company counted all nationalities, though a great part of the body were French, Germans and Russians. I was the only American. There were Poles, Italians, Austrians, Hungarians, Greeks, Arabs, Spaniards. There was even a negro —but not an American negro. His name was Ahlmadu; he was a little negro from Sierra Leone, a British colony on the coast of Africa, and he spoke English fluently, with the accent of a British lord. Common language drew us together in those first hurly-burly days with our new, strange and rough companions; little Ahlmadu was my nearest friend in those first hard days. He is dead now: after going through all the fighting and coming out of it like a cat with nine lives, he was stabbed to death just a little while ago, in a brawl in a café of Marseilles, over a "lady."

Out of the one hundred and twenty men making up the company, we were thirty *bleus*, blue ones, as the recruits are called. The other ninety were old salted-down Legionaires nearing the end of their terms of enlistment, and the more reckless for it, and some of them were right out of the prison, and all of them held picturesque service records larded with citations for insubordination, absence without leave, intoxication, fighting, selling equipment, all the peccadillos of the service, but not one of them, you may believe, for cowardice. They were a hard, brawling, tough, dissolute lot, that bunch into which we thirty *bleus* were thrown, and we had a time to hold our own; but demons for fighting we found them, and good comrades in stress and combat. Among the *bleus* was a blond, blue-eyed Pole, named Sylvestre Budney, who later was to become my *copain*, my "buddy."

A company of the Legion is usually commanded, of course, by a captain. But so costly had been the losses in officers of late, what with the fighting in Morocco and Syria, that a lieutenant commanded us. He was a slim, stoop-shouldered Frenchman, Vernon by name, with a brilliant war record, holding the Legion of Honor and the Croix de Guerre. He was hard, as they all are in the Legion, but just, tireless in caring for his men, brave as they make them and always ready to share risk and peril. He soon gained a remarkable ascendancy over his wild crew. He spoke perfect

English, and as he had a way of singling out men now and then for a moment's talk, often spoke to me in my native tongue. He was killed at Suweida, and there is not a man of his hard-boiled bunch who would not have gone into hell rather than see him die.

The work of organizing the company went steadily on; there was plenty to do. We were equipped anew in every detail from head to foot and went about, carrying and putting away our stuff, pleased as children coming from the Christmas tree. Finally we were reviewed and notified we were leaving the next morning.

We had been sleeping in the stables, as there was no room in the barracks. At an ungodly hour we rolled our packs, had coffee and marched over to the main *carré* for pay, rations and muster. Then the company was lined up by sections, roll was called, and "en avant" we marched to the station. We were headed by the *Clique* with its fifes, drums, trumpets and bugles while a guard of honor followed us. The *Clique* rang out with its best pieces, its gayest, most rhythmic airs, drawing us along at the Legion's rapid marching step; windows opened as we passed, arms waved, and we felt a great thrill.

At the station, we lined up for parade, and Colonel Rollet arrived to inspect us and bid us good-by. As was his way, he walked slowly along the entire line, examining the equipment of each man, speaking a few words to each, searching each pair of eyes with his own terrible blue ones. Then we presented arms, went rapidly through the manual. The guard of honor in its turn presented arms in salute to us, the *Clique* struck up the March of the Legion, and we embarked upon the train.

For six days, on our way to Bizerte, we were rolled on that train, and to this day I can look back upon this bit of touring with absolute horror. The cars we were in were coaches, old coaches of the continental type, cut up into hermetic compartments. Each compartment was supposed in regular service to seat eight squeezed civilians in the rare case when it might be *complet*. Well, ours were *complets* from the first; eight of us forced themselves into each compartment. And we were not civilians, but soldiers, thick with our uniforms and overcoats, carrying rifle and bayonet, *bidon* and *musette*, bed roll and pack. We were packed like sardines; we could not stir, and the heat was terrible. The country was mountainous;

every now and then the train crawled into a tunnel; we were bathed in steam and choking sulphurous smoke, we suffocated and nearly died.

Of course there was no room to stretch, to lie down. Six days and six nights thus; we slept, when we slept at all, sitting up, wedged upright between our fellows.

The old Legionaires snored, fought, tried to play cards, abused the *bleus*, but most of all exercised their ingenuity in the getting of wine. This, I was soon to learn, was the Vingt-neuvième's most intense preoccupation. At every station on the way, as we stopped, guards would immediately be posted to keep the men from running out in search of wine. As well try to hold a thousand rabbits as the one hundred twenty men of the Vingt-neuvième. Never have I seen such ingenuity displayed, such imagination and such gay craft as by these Legionaires bent upon having wine. In spite of the strict orders, in spite of the posted guards, at each station the *bidons* found themselves replenished as if by magic. I was between two Russians, old Legionaires; every now and then across me they would start a fight—fights were breaking out, of course, continuously the whole length of the train—and I, remembering I was but a *bleu*, kept pretty quiet in my own small portion of the compartment.

And on the fourth day I received my first wound, the only one I ever received in the Legion, and that was not from a bullet.

We had come to a little switching station, a mere tank in the desert, and as is done for mysterious reasons on railroads all over the world, they began to switch us around. This was not supposed to be a stop so we were being kept in the cars. We went back and forth, pulled by the little puffing engine and its Arab driver; back and forth, back and forth, and bang, bang, bang. Finally our car stopped and was still, and I put my head out at the compartment window to see if I could find out what it all was about.

I chose exactly the right moment. Or it may have been that Arab driver was laying for me. Anyway, just then, debouching enthusiastically out of a little spur, he came along the main line and with his locomotive hit our car a smart rap.

My head was through the window. It did not move as fast as did the window frame around it; and a side of it hit me a dreadful whack across the eye. The shock threw me on my back in the middle of the compartment, and then, from the luggage nets above, the packs, the rifles and the bayonets of my comrades came down upon me, finishing the engine-driver's job.

How I bled! A little bright fountain was geysering from the cut just above the eye. It was, of course, compared especially to things I was to see later, quite a minor injury, but spectacular it was. Lieutenant Vernon came running to me as they got me out, full of an almost amusing concern. First aid packs were ripped, I was daubed with stinging iodine, then bandaged.

This made my discomfort complete. My eye swelled and swelled and finally closed. It looked like a bad eye indeed. For a time I was afraid I was going to lose it. The army doctor who treated me when we had reached Bizerte would shake his head despondently over it. "But, but, but, I don't understand," he would exclaim. "Just a cut, a clean cut, well treated, why should it act like that?" He seemed to consider the extraordinary conduct of the eye as a base betrayal, a low form of attack on his professional reputation. "I don't understand, I don't understand, at all," he would assure me—which was not reassuring. The eye finally got well, and I now bear a scar of this, the only wound I have been able to collect out of two wars and I don't know how many battles.

For the week we were in Bizerte, awaiting ship, the bad eye acted as a mentor and moderator and held me relatively quiet, which was probably a good thing. For the Vingt-neuvième Compagnie, after that fine start of the train, was holding the pace. During the day we were busy, of course, as only the Legionaire is kept busy. But between five and nine we roamed the town. By some unfortunate arrangement a canteen was down the road just a little way from our barracks, and there wine was sold at fourteen cents (about three of ours) a bottle; and all the old veterans of our company, because of the extra fighting pay that now came to them, felt rich. Usually they had a good start before they reached town. And there they engaged in the games and pastimes which suit their rather rough sense of humor. They were also getting their first taste of the native *raké* compared to which cognac is like sweet milk. Fights broke out continuously here and there, wherever any gathered; bottles flew through the air, furniture was wrecked. A bottle fight is the Legionaire's greatest joy when *en permission*, next to evading or actually assaulting the detachments of military police which patrol such garrison cities, and which are doubled or tripled or quadrupled when the Legion is known to be their guest. Wherever it is, something is always flying—if not bullets, it's bottles.

What makes the Legionaires dangerous customers in affrays of all kinds is that same esprit de corps which makes them so redoubtable in battle. "The Legionaires always stick together." They say that and they do it. You rarely see a Legionaire roaming a city alone; they go by groups of two, three, four, or five. And it is incredible, if trouble comes to any of these groups, how swiftly, as if by magic, other groups arrive, till a small nucleus of misunderstanding or quarrel swells into a big roiled mob of fighting men. In this the Legionaire in incorrigible. Heavy penalties are inflicted upon him. But what is eight or nine days of prison to a Legionaire, compared to the traditions of his famous corps? Eight days? He takes it with a shrug. "J' m'en fiche," he says, only it isn't *fiche* he says, but the more vigorous and martial verb.

Already our company, so lately formed, and of such mixed elements, had become welded by the fire of Legion tradition. We came into a peaceful

Bizerte, full of well-behaved troops, of artillerymen, tirailleurs and zouaves amenable to discipline; in a trice we had made of the place a wild bedlam.

Finally, at the end of eight days, we received orders to leave the next day. We were embarking for Beirut, for Syria and the fighting.

We were *consignés* all this day, that is, held in quarters, and all the next night, so that we would be fresh and in good condition in the morning, and make of our sailing, at least, something of a credit to us. A special program had been arranged for the embarkation in the morning, a little ceremony meant to give dignity and meaning and the proper undertone of patriotic gravity to our departure.

Everything went well at first. We lined up in the morning with the *Clique* and the fanfare at the head. "Epaulez—armes!" our lieutenant cried, and off we went behind the gay music and the screaming bugles, eyes straight ahead, arms swinging, stepping it fast in exact rhythm, as noble-looking an outfit as is ever seen. Every one turned as we passed and windows opened, for there was now no doubt as to where we were going.

We halted in a big beautiful square facing the dock, and here were many officers, and a guard of honor, and the massed bands of the Tirailleurs which presently struck up the March of the Legion. The embarkation was evidently going to be a noble show. And then the Vingt-neuvième's irresistible *penchant* for the wine that is red spoiled everything.

We had been *consignés* a day and a night, and since early morning a special patrol had watched us and severely barred all liquid communications. Even now this special patrol hung vigilant about us.

But the ship which was to take us was not yet at the dock. The order "sac à terre" was given and we crossed our bayonets, slipped our packs to the pavement, and sat upon them. The idea was that we should thus rest quietly till the ship was in, then resume our military bearing and burden, and to the sounds of music, alertly embark in a fine show of disciplined order.

But the Vingt-neuvième seemed to have the power of sucking wine to itself. Here we sat in the center of an open square. There stood the vigilant dry patrol. Yet little by little, mysteriously, as if by some natural infiltration, wine began to appear among the men. A little rivulet at first—then a river, then rivers. *Bidons* passed about, mouths were being wiped with backs of hands.

When the ship had finally docked, and time came for our planned departure with full *panache*, the Vingt-neuvième Compagnie du Premier Régiment Etrangère was unable to rise to the occasion. The massed bands of the Tirailleurs struck up the Marche de la Légion once more, the guard of honor presented arms.

But half of the company could walk only in zigzags and lurches, and fully twenty men could not walk at all. To those of us who could walk it fell to get those who could not walk aboard. Instead of marching briskly up the gang-plank in single file, we went by threes. Two, more or less sober, bearing their rifles, their packs, all their equipment, and moreover, the distributed pack and equipment of a third, would start up the plank with that third one between them. Sometimes he would be completely inert, and went along with feet dragging, like a dead man; sometimes he harbored still signs of life, and, in the firm grasp of his comrades, gestured like a puppet in wild farewell gestures toward the shore.

A fine sight it was. Lieutenant Vernon was tearing his hair at this result of all his efforts. Thus it was the Vingt-neuvième went off to war.

CHAPTER V

THE four days at sea, steaming through the Ægean, past islands—Cyprus, Crete, and so on—which up to that time had existed for me only in books, were a nice recess after the hard period of training we had just passed. Our quarters on board the transport were airy and clean; the bunks between decks comfortable. The weather was hot but fine; hour after hour we slid over a still blue sea. Gradually even those of the Legionaires who had the worst cases of "mal aux cheveux" from the embarking celebration recovered, shook themselves, began to look for new worlds to conquer.

I was gradually fitting myself into my new world, and making acquaintances among my fellows. I had found some Legionaires who spoke a little English—a German and a Norwegian. I talked a lot with the little negro Ahlmadu, with his almost Oxford accent. Also I was fast picking up some French, though it was a sort of blind French, since I only heard the words and did not know what they looked like.

Some regular artillery was on board, its men mostly young French boys. We *bleus* of the Legion and these boys spent many hours listening to tales from the old Legionaires—old bearded fellows, baked and rebaked by the African sun, gnarled from the hardships of many campaigns. Their favorite stories were of the late fierce fighting in Morocco, and these were not only naturally of high color, but rather daubed to impress us. We sprawled on the moonlit deck around the old fellows, and listened with eyes wide and ears pricked forward. In return we'd invite the chronicler to a turn at the canteen, which he would accept with dignity and indulgence.

Our duties were light. A few hours of guard duty now and then; everything was peace. And finally on the fourth day we saw land. At first the mountains. They stretched, seemingly, away up in the sky, a line of sad khaki-colored hills, mangy and bare, with something about them harsh and ominous. The desert land at their foot gradually came to view, and finally Beirut, a blinding white city from the ship, with the streets showing like black bars.

Meanwhile the ruling passion of the Vingt-neuvième de Marche had fermented and bubbled again. To be just, the beginning lay with the artillery. A corporal of the artillery detachment on board had found in the hold a barrel of rum, had dextrously tapped it. Artillery *bidons* were passing down there in an endless chain, and coming up filled.

It was not long, of course, before the Vingt-neuvième, with its special and highly cultivated flair, found out what was doing. Their *bidons* began to slide down to the wounded barrel in the hold and to come up filled.

Now the *bidon* is no thin hip flask, but a solid and rotund vessel holding just two liters, which is a little more than two quarts. And the rum in the barrel was issue rum, the "tafia" which in the French army is held in reserve for desperate occasions, when men are utterly worn out or freezing with the cold, when a few drops doled out restore as if by magic the body and the morale, and turn the exhausted man from a rag to a tiger. Not by the drop were the Legionaires drinking it now; they frankly upheld their heavy *bidons* to the sky and let a live stream gurgle down their throats. In no time we were as we had been at our remarkable embarkation. Songs were being bawled, quarrels were breaking out everywhere; down upon the roisterers the sergeants would storm, with threats and punishments, trying to quell the disorder or keep it down at least, as a man tries to hold escaping steam by sitting down on a valve.

All night as we lay at anchor before the city, the disorder and the din kept up. It was a beautiful night, with the full moon up; I know that because I was on guard that night—a double period, too, as in some way I was forgotten by the first relief. My job was to guard the companionway between the Legion's quarters and the canteen, and it proved some job, too, leaving me little time to dream or to watch the sleeping oriental city under the moon. Every now and then some black shadow came crawling along like an Indian, then rose with a yell and tried to rush by me to the canteen. Or a lurching Legionaire, as if he did not know what he was doing, would bump heavily against me, and while I was thus engaged, another, or two or three, would try to rush by. Or a peaceful-looking fellow would start a gentle conversation, under the cover of which his *copain* tried to worm by like a movie-picture *peau-rouge*. And these were all old Legionaires, and I was only a *bleu*.

At sunrise we disembarked. General Sarrail,

famous of the World War and military governor of Syria, reviewed us to music. Out of the corners of our eyes we could see the roofs and the minarets of Beirut, and remembering Bizerte promised ourselves a good time. And then we were marched right straight through the center of the city and out again by the other side! And thence on to a camp by the beach seven kilometers away. The authorities knew the Vingt-neuvième by this time.

We remained all day at the camp by the sea, looking longingly toward the city and its promises. And at four-thirty in the afternoon, were marched back, again through the city, with its whirl of color, its cafés and its bazars, out through the other side, and on—a quick forced march of seven kilometers with no rest, to the station where our train was waiting for us. We were on our way toward those ominous khaki-colored hills we had seen in the morning from the ship.

We traveled, as usual, in compartments crowded to suffocation. But it was not hot long. As the train, curling and zigzagging, climbed up into the hills, it became bitterly cold. Night shut down. I had learned something, and slept stretched on the floor, between the feet of my comrades.

By four or five o'clock, when the dawn came, we were going through a high pass. Out of the windows we could see now and then a few small stone houses, and inhabitants of the country, shivering in their sheepskin coats. There were barbed wire entanglements, every house was loop-holed, and spahis with their white turbans and Syrians with their red and purple fezzes, guarded the track. Then the train curved down into a beautiful valley, and we saw the yellow walls, the minarets, the gardens of Damascus.

Unworthy suspicion still hovered over the Vingt-neuvième. We were not allowed into the town at all, but kept at the station at a distance. Soldiers were everywhere—Syrians, tirailleurs, chasseurs, spahis; and artillery, and transports and *automobiles blindés*, as they call their armored cars. There was great stir and bustle, and excitement in the air.

We got out, had breakfast, stretched our legs, filled our *bidons* (with water this time), took on chocolate, *pâté* and *singe* for the mid-day *déjeuner*. A new train pulled in, and this time it was an armored train. We loaded five machine-guns on it, and a sixty-five millimeter field gun, and embarked.

The tracks were now closely guarded, every now and then we passed a patrol of spahis on their fiery little horses, colorful in their white turbans and long flowing burnous and big baggy trousers, and their funny saddles like rocking-chairs. Now and then we stopped at some post to revictual it. They were virtually in state of siege, surrounded with barbed wire and trenches, all the walls loopholed. On the flat roof above always a sentinel stood, anxiously scanning with his binoculars the hills from which the Druses descended. Their razzias of late had been frequent, several posts had been surprised at night and annihilated. The garrisons were of tirailleurs or Senegalese. The Senegalese wore their little red tasseled caps, and beside their rifles carried their "coupe-coupe," a big knife without any point, a sort of glorified butcher's cleaver of which they are very fond, and with which they are supposed to do great execution, having a childish fondness for heads.

These posts were along the railroad, which ran a course parallel to the hills, winding in and out of them and exposed along its whole line to the Druse descents from their heights. At all there was an atmosphere of worry and tension.

At last we came to Ezraa, central post of the line. Here were a supply base, a field hospital, and a high signal tower, and batteries of artillery ready for action. In the distance lay a long, low, blue range of grim mountains. I asked one of the native troops what it was and he said, "the Jebel Druse range."

Then he pointed to a particular peak of the mountains, and finally I saw what looked like a little white spot flashing up there in the sun. "Suweida," he said. "A *poste*. Sieged by the Druses."

That little post up in the mountain had been cut off for days but was still bravely fighting. And even as I stood there, from the top of the high observation tower, above my head, they began to heliograph to it. A moment later, afar off up there, I saw the brave little tiny solar winkings of its answer. What did it answer? I did not know. Perhaps "All is well," or perhaps a despairing S. O. S.

The train went on. More posts, all heavily armed, all alert, all worried. Then we came to a station with just a few houses and a camp, and a big shout arose. "The Legion!" we shouted. We were all tired of seeing artillerymen, tirailleurs, Syrians, spahis, and Senegalese. Here was a camp of Legionaires; we were home.

How did we know right away they were Legionaires? By their kepi, the sacred kepi. There was little else of their equipment that was revelatory; these men shouting at us were stripped to the waist! But they had on their kepis, worn at the exact angle.

To the kepi—scarlet and blue in peace time, khaki-colored in war—the Legion clings as it clings to all its traditions, stubbornly. Effort after effort has been made to provide them with a top piece that will shield them better from the sun; they will have none of them; even against orders they will cling to their kepi, which, as a matter of fact, worn at the right angle, accurately expresses the half-sardonic, rough *insouciance* of the Legionaire. On this campaign we had been issued cork helmets. We would not wear them; we forgot them, we lost them whenever we could. Or, when being sniped, held them up till they were full of holes. I remember going back to camp from the firing line with a Legionaire who amused himself with his helmet as if it were a football, kicking and dribbling it all the way back to the camp, and there finishing the game by a last boot which sent the remains into an abandoned trench. To the sergeant's question the next day about the helmet he negligently answered that it had been shot off his head.

Now men with kepis, most of them stripped to the waist, for they had been toiling, came pouring out of the camp toward the train. Men on the train were recognizing old comrades out there, men outside were shouting to old friends on the train. For a moment everything seemed mixed in a swirl of recognition, slaps on the shoulder and jubilation. But soon, having left the train, we re-formed, marched into the camp, and made our own by its side.

The way camp is made in the Legion is thus. The three sections of our company were marched upon the chosen *terrain* in three files, with a wide interval between them. Within the files, of course, were the proper intervals between the squads, consisting each of five men and a corporal. At the word "halt," the three sections stopped. Then each corporal (which meant every sixth man) raised his bayonet on high. The *ad-*

judant-chef, passing at the head of each section-file in turn, rectified the positions till along each file the raised bayonets were exactly in line. Then to his bawled order each corporal lowered his bayonet, and thrust it into the ground.

Now all over the area of the camp were bayonets equally spaced, and where each bayonet was stuck a tent was raised.

The tents, in the Legion, shelter each six men. They are carried in the packs, one to each squad. The pickets and the ropes are also evenly distributed in the packs, so that the Legion carries its house on its back.

In a trice we had the tents up, our *paquetages* arranged within; then came the dreaded cry, "Aux murailles!"

This meant that a wall was to be built—the hardest labor there is, and one which the Legionaire cordially loathes. Yet whenever we made camp in hostile country we had to do it—and often during the night, were glad we had done it.

The place for the wall was marked, completely encircling the camp. Twenty men, the masons, were detailed here to do the actual setting of the stones. And the rest of us were sent out to get them and bring them in.

It was exhausting toil under a broiling sun, and seemingly without end. I carried in, I wager, hundreds of stones weighing from twenty pounds up and mostly up, torn bitterly out of the very earth. Each time we came in with our stones, we measured with our eyes the rising wall. It did not seem to be rising at all; we thought it would never be breast high. But it actually began to rise. It was ankle high, it was knee high, it was waist high. It seemed to stick there a great while. And suddenly it was finished. It was breast high, the regulation height. "Bien," said the sergeant.

But the wall had been built with a break at regular intervals to allow, of course, for egress. Now, outside of each of these openings, a smaller wall must be built. More lugging of stones. Then when that was finished, we must put up barbed-wire entanglements outside.

Finally that was done, and we returned to the wall and made our loopholes, our *créneaux*.

Each man made his own *créneau*, or loophole, according to his height, his conformation, his taste or even his caprice, and after that it was *his créneau*, no one else's, his to run to in case of an *alerte*, his from which to shoot. Woe to him who, in the confusion of a night attack, made for the wrong one. Each man his own *créneau*, that's the rule of the Legion.

I suppose that the Romans of old built just such camps as we built that day.

What interested me most about the building of the camp was what was done for the horses and the mules. The wall, of course, is built breast high so as to afford a shield to the sleeping men from the bullets of snipers or the volleys of sudden razzias. But we had with us, in our outfit, the horses of the officers, and some twenty pack mules. And horses and mules are, of course, higher than breast high. How were they going to be protected, the precious mules?

Well, an *écurie* was made for them in the very center of the camp. And the ground was dug, under their feet, till slowly they had sunk below the level of the protective walls, with only the tips of the mules' long ears perhaps showing.

This meant more digging. I was beginning to understand why the French often refer to the Legion as "un enfer."

That night—after this well-spent day—I had my first experience at standing guard in hostile country. Fixed sentinels were posted about thirty feet apart, with mobile sentinels to pace between them. The fixed sentinel stands still, looking straight ahead over the sector in his keeping. Behind him the mobile sentinel paces, linking the fixed guards. The fixed sentinel hears him coming, feels him behind him. "Rien à signaller?" asks the mobile sentinel's voice; and the fixed sentinel answers "Rien" if there indeed is nothing, or, if suspicious of some dim shadow, some uncertain noise, tells him of it.

I was a fixed sentinel that night. It was a beautiful calm night, very cold, and during my two hours a crescent of moon shone. I was, of course, this being my first time at it, extremely serious about it, and not a little nervous. And there were plenty of sounds to make the heart beat. The bubbling and munching of camels in the shadows. The sudden crying out of jackals, like the screams of a woman being slowly murdered. And near dawn an Arab on a flat roof suddenly filled the stillness with his high-pitched, gabbling prayer. Once I saw a shadow crawling—but it was only a shadow.

CHAPTER VI

For eight days we were in Ghazalé, living the camp life, which if a bit relaxed was a busy life. The walls we had put up in such a hurry were strengthened still more for we were in dangerous country; the Druses were attacking posts everywhere, and just a month before, an entire French column of four thousand men had been practically annihilated, with two thousand of its men killed.

The *géneral-en-chef* decided of a fine morning there should be a nice aviation field at Bosra, so we were of course put at it. This meant more stone work like that for the wall. Every stone must be picked off the field, then the uneven places filled in. Joyous work, under the broiling sun. We went about stripped to the waist, getting as black as Arabs.

When this was done we had a little respite. We did some drill in extended order; the rest of the time was given to washing our clothes, keeping our equipment in order, and in the different *corvées.*

Of these, the principal were getting water and getting wood. Kitchens, by the way, had been built against the walls. In the Legion there is a kitchen and a cook to each section. The cook of my section was a Frenchman from Marseilles, land of the bouilleabaisse, and was a fine cook, often getting wonderful returns out of the stern rations.

Every day some of us were detailed to bring in water or bring in wood. It was a half kilometer to water—a well to which had been fitted a gasoline pump which filled a great trough. To this trough came the water-getters of all the other outfits, and the native women of the village population, the automobile convoys, armored cars, and long camel trains. The scene was a colored bedlam.

We of the *corvée* would go out there, each carrying two canvas pails, and twenty of the big heavy two-liter *bidons*. In addition, of course, we carried our rifles, for we were under orders to go nowhere unarmed, the Druses and their followers having a fondness for cutting the throats of lone unarmed men. The *bidons* we strapped to our waists, the rifle we slung over the shoulder, and we carried the buckets.

There at the well, we would find bedlam—everybody fighting for place, and the camels impartially biting at any one in reach of their long, yellow, flat infected teeth. The pretty part of the picture was given by the Syrian women, who looked like colored pictures out of the Bible. They bore their water on top of their heads, walking gracefully beneath the load. The vessels they bore so majestically upon their heads though were discarded gasoline cans of the Standard Oil Company.

The women of that country are closely guarded. Pretty as many were, it was difficult to hazard any love-making. But in the Legion, as everywhere, there are the managing boys who solve all difficulties.

Well, each man would place his twenty *bidons* into line, and in this pushing and swirling crowd, would try to fill them from the buckets dipped in the trough. Our difficulties were increased from the fact that every outfit was trying to steal every other's *bidons*. From a *corvée* I returned one day with two *bidons* missing—and one of them was my sergeant's. He *sacrebleu*'d me to a fare-thee-well, called me all sorts of an animal, and ended by commanding me to return next day without fail with the two *bidons*. Not yet being quite used to the ways of the Legion, I was in a quandary. But Delaporte, one of the bad eggs of my section, seeing my difficulty, cheerfully offered his services. "I'll get them," he said eagerly. He disappeared for a while and reappeared bearing two strange *bidons*, which he gave me, and which in turn I gave to the sergeant, who accepted them as a matter of course. The "*sous-off*" of the Legion is great at giving an order without bothering himself at all as to how it is carried out. "Je m'en fiche," he says for that part of it, only it isn't quite *fiche* that he says.

The *corvée* of the wood was a more joyful occasion. At this camp we were supposed to be able to get wood brought in by the railroad. But there never was any, or there never was enough, so we had to forage for it, and the villages suffered. We would "borrow," taking wood away with promises to bring the equivalent back—which of course we would, and could, never do. We dug up fences, posts, in the darkness without asking permission. One of our men came in from the *corvée* one night with an entire door which he had unhinged without the owners' knowledge.

They were sleeping at the very moment innocently, in a house without a door. One quickly adapts himself to the customs of the country. I remember taking away a gate, on a main street, in broad daylight. In this as in other things the officers' attitude was the same. They'd give the order. As to the method of execution, "blanketyvous" they said, using a word I cannot translate, first because its English equivalent is too mild for the exact effect, and secondly because even that milder equivalent would with difficulty get by in the United States mail.

Our pleasures were those of the Legion when campaigning. The inhabitants of the country were friendly here. They were Syrian peasants. They wore a kind of smock, baggy bloomers, and on their heads a square of colored cloth, blue, red, or black, tied into a sort of turban by a braid of camel hair. They raised wheat in little fields between the stones. And we could always get tomatoes, onions and dates. And wonderful grapes, the best I have ever tasted, could be bought very cheap. For half a franc they almost filled your kepi; for a franc they would fill it to the brim.

There were of course other pleasures of less idyllic character. Canteens had been set up near the camp. They follow the armies—till it is too close to the bullets. They were usually kept by Greeks, and were semi-official in that they must get permission from the commander of the unit near which they set up their stores. This, of course, was a necessity wherever the Legion went. Three fourths of those wild fellows would have deserted if they had no drink and none of the rough pleasures that go with the canteen.

So they spent their few hours of leisure after hard labor in the canteen, drinking and, many of them, gambling. The games most popular with them were chemin-de-fer, vingt-et-un, and a game they called minee-et-dinee, from the German words *mein* and *dein* which mean mine and yours. This was the simplest game I ever saw; cards reduced to the first elements. You drew a card, your opponent drew a card; whoever had the highest card copped the bet. A simple game, and also a swift one, at which one could lose an astonishing amount of one's pay in an astonishingly short time.

And then, of course, they got drunk a good deal, the old Legionaires. The Vingt-neuvième had been put together with veterans who were not exactly timid young girls or winged angels.

They would get drunk, and some of them were particularly ugly when drunk.

There was Gorigas, for instance, of my section. He was a wild, irresponsible monkey, a tough egg and bad actor. When drunk he would terrorize the canteen.

There was one man in the whole outfit who could handle Gorigas in his cups, and that was Sergeant d'Etienne. Whenever men would come to the lieutenant, and say, "*Mon lieutenant*, Gorigas has broken out in the canteen; he has his knife out and is threatening to cut everybody's throat," Sergeant d'Etienne would be sent for.

He would go to the canteen, enter, and go quietly to Gorigas, as he roared there, waving his knife. "*Tiens*, Gorigas!" he would say in a tone of surprise. "How about *un petit coup*—a little drink."

"*Ah, mon sergent!*" Gravely Gorigas would have a drink with the sergeant.

"*Maintenant, à mon tour*. Now, it's my turn." And Gorigas would treat the sergeant.

This formality over, Sergeant d'Etienne would say softly, "Now come, Gorigas."

And Gorigas would go along with him and back to camp, mild as a lamb.

If any one else had come near him at such a time, he would have slashed him with his knife.

Others were of the same temperament, unapproachable when drunk. Delaporte, the restorer of my *bidons*, was of such. These men in that state would savagely attack any one who came near them. I myself was lucky in having a bit of that which was possessed by Sergeant d'Etienne. I was never set upon by any of these men. But I have seen others take merciless beatings. When they fight in the Legion it is not according to Marquis of Queensberry rules. Toward the Marquis the average Legionaire has only a very far and hardly bowing acquaintance. In a Legion fight, bayonets are apt to be drawn, knives to flash. Bottles as clubs or projectiles are very popular, and usually the chairs and the tables follow the bottles. At the best hobnailed boots that stamp, hands that strangle, fingers that gouge, supplement the fist. I have even seen teeth used. And there exist no exaggerated scruples against ganging. Two or three will sometimes unite against one. But let any Legionaire be attacked by any outsider, and it is the whole Legion which is then the gang. "La légion! La légion!" Your hear a hoarse bawl in some blind alley—

and immediately the sound of running feet. It is the Legion rallying in defense of its own.

The queer ascendancy that Sergeant d'Etienne possessed over Gorigas, Delaporte and others of his ilk had this result as far as I was concerned. All of the desperadoes were placed in his section, and it happened to be my section! I was in fine company indeed. In my own squad, only two of us were *bleus* or recruits: myself and Sylvestre Budney, a young Pole. To protect ourselves against the exactions of the four others, who being old Legionaires up on the traditions of the body took delight in hazing and bullying the *bleus*, we formed a defensive alliance, which worked well and saved us much.

Beside the canteen keepers, there were other camp-followers, of another sex. I mention this only because I have pledged myself to tell the whole truth in this book. This also was a semi-official institution in that only the girls who subjected themselves to periodic physical examination were allowed near the camps. In the buildings harboring these girls the worst fights and riots occurred.

While we were in Ghazalé we took part in a little expedition which resembled rent collecting.

The French divided villages into the villages *soumis*, which accepted their authority, and the villages *insoumis*, considered in revolt. And one of the tests in the classification was the willing payment of taxes.

About twelve kilometers from us, on the edge of the Druse country, there was a village which had refused to pay taxes, and which was suspected of harboring Druse spies and giving them news of our movements. In the middle of the night, we silently marched off toward this village to collect.

Some of the old Legionaires were elated. They had heard rare things of such expeditions. They knew that if the tax was still refused, in spite of such formal asking, then everything in the village was taken and the houses burned. This meant loot. You returned with goats, sheep, horses and chicken; sometimes if you were lucky, with trinkets, linen and silk. There were stories of men having found jewelry, of another having found a pot of gold coins. The old devils of my section wet their lips with anticipation. Not that they were misers, apt to hoard gold. But gold meant lots of wine and plenty of dancing girls.

We set out at dead of night, covered by a

squadron of Legion cavalry and a squadron of mounted spahis. We reached the village at dawn. It was a mountain aery, with high walls like those of a medieval castle, up on a crest. We surrounded it silently while the cavalry guarded us. On heights about we could see mounted Druses, watching for a second, then disappearing, galloping into sight again, and again vanishing like a cavalry of ghosts.

The major of the battalion, Major Pratzert, was in command of the operation. He arrived in his auto—together with an *officier* of *renseignements*, an intelligence officer well versed in the country, and, together with a small patrol, they went right into the village and disappeared.

We waited a long time on the qui vive, freezing in the morning wind, with the ghostly riders watching us from the hills. In spite of the growls of the "*sous-off's*" the men talked. They wondered impatiently what was happening. Bets were laid. They hoped the village notables would refuse to pay the taxes, so that we could do a little looting.

And then the major came out with the emir of the village, and two men with the tax money in a bag!

My comrades felt gypped. They let out a growl. A fine result after getting up so early in the morning and tramping all this way. "*Quelle sacrée vie!* What a h— of a life!"

We marched back, disconsolate. The expedition had been a success from the point of view of the French Government; from the point of view of the Legionaire it was an expedition completely *raté*—a dead loss.

CHAPTER VII

WHEN we had been in camp in Ghazalé eight days, we received orders to march to the village of Mousseifré. We were to build an advanced post there and to hold it at all cost. The two companies of Legionaires we had joined in Ghazalé were now with us, and together we formed a battalion.

The march proved to be one of eighteen kilometers, right across the *bled*, along the edge of the hills. We tramped in sand with our heavy packs, the heat was terrific, there was no water on the way.

Mousseifré we found much different from Ghazalé. We had now pointed deep into the war zone. It was a sad collection of flat-topped houses with a mosque at the center. The remnants of the miserable population regarded us with sullen suspicion. We soon were to learn that they were hand in glove with the enemy, and spies that gave the Druses full information as to our movements and our strength.

Whatever water we had here was brought to us from a distance on camels. It was the worst water I had ever seen. It "was crawling and it stunk." When thirst forced us to drink, we filtered it from our *bidons* through our handkerchiefs—and found worms in our handkerchiefs.

We had no sooner arrived than sounded the dreaded cry, "Aux murailles!"

This time we did not build one stone-walled camp as we had at Bosra. We built six small ones, that completely surrounded the town, and one in the center. The camps were far enough apart so that the enemy, charging the village, would be enfiladed. There were two sections to each camp. The commandant and his état-major established themselves in a fortified stone house near the mosque, and the squadron of cavalry that accompanied us—Legion cavalry, in which were many Cossacks—were quartered within the village. Each camp was an independent unit able to take care of itself. Within, each man, with his *créneau*, had about fifteen feet to hold. There was a dearth of barbed wire, so all we could put up in front of the walls was one thin line of it.

How we toiled here, putting up these walls! The heat was terrific and we had little water.

There was no shade anywhere, and the insides of the tents were like furnaces. Our allowance of water was four *bidons* a day of the vile stinking stuff. Half of that went to the kitchens. This left a man four liters a day to keep his clothes clean, drink, wash his face and shave. We didn't shave. Neither did we wash our faces much. As a matter of fact, we lost half of our water trying to strain it. We became a horrible-looking lot, with bristling beards and matted hair. The air was always full of sand; we were dirty, all except for our rifles. These we were eternally cleaning.

After putting up the wall, there came the usual order to clean up a landing field for planes. We picked all the stones up off an enormous area, filled up holes; we were groggy with work and, stripped to the waist, looked like bandits.

From where we were, we now had a clear view of the besieged post of Suweida, farther up into the hills. What had seemed to me, the first time I had seen it from the railroad, not much more than a white spot gleaming in the sun, now showed as a town with high walls, on a crest. And in the center of it the besieged citadel rose, high and white, with the little tricolor flag, no bigger than a handkerchief from where we stood, ever waving in the breeze, almost gaily. We were ever in communication with the garrison, by heliograph at day and lamp blinker at night. Nearly all the time as we toiled, we could see their tiny winkings. We men of the rank did not know the meaning of most of these messages, but the defenders were known to be hard pressed, and we imagined sometimes tragic ones—we are getting out of water, we have no more food, the wounded are suffering, and so on. Some of the messages would have almost immediate effect. From Ghazalé, planes laden with bombs came flapping over our heads, and on up to the post, where we could see them drop their loads all around the citadel. Columns of dust and smoke rose up there, concealing everything; both town and citadel were hidden as if in a tornado.

On the day after the arrival of our battalion in Mousseifré, we made our first reconnaissance. Opposite our camp was a hill, and on the other side of it was an abandoned village, which had been half destroyed by the bombs of the aviators. A detachment was sent up over the hill, into the village and beyond to observe the movements of the enemy. This patrol consisted of one of our three companies, the nineteenth, and of a squadron of cavalry; the Vingt-neuvième remained in camp.

The detachment disappeared over the hill, we could not see what was happening. After a while we heard some hot firing over there, and later the detachment returned with several wounded men and the body of a dead sergeant lying across a saddle. It seemed that they had run into strong bodies of the enemy over there, and a hot fire. The lieutenant in charge had wisely declined to push things too far and had extricated his men. The sergeant had been shot right out of the saddle by a bullet which had pierced his brain. We buried him a little way from the camp, putting up over him a little cross with his kepi hung on it.

This action electrified the camp; we knew now we were in a real row. That night guards were tripled, the machine-gun men slept beside their pieces, and, as did all the Legionaires, I slept along the wall, right beneath my *créneau*, my rifle strapped to my arm, a little heap of grenades at my feet.

We always slept with our rifles strapped to our arms in such country, for the Druses were adroit and tireless at crawling into camps at night, to snatch from some careless man his rifle and make away with it, incidentally leaving the late owner with his throat neatly cut. And we were not satisfied to have them strapped to our arms; we literally slept on them.

Within our low and hastily built walls, we were two sections, with two machine-guns, about seventy men in all. Each of the other small redoubts held about the same number of men. In the town was the commandant and his état-major, fortified in a barbed-wired stone house near the mosque, and the cavalry in another redoubt. We were about six hundred men in all at the most.

At three-thirty in the morning, a sergeant making his round of the outposts thought he heard a stone rattle on the slope before the camp, in the direction of the enemy. He put his ear to the ground and heard a rumor of rolling stones, and the grunting of camels. "Aux armes!" he bellowed.

The cry was taken up and passed along, and we rose to our feet, at our *créneaux*, shoved our guns through, and were ready in the black and bitterly cold night. Nothing happened for a time.

The night before, we had been awakened by a

false alarm. A little Portuguese, no bigger than a minute, a bit foolish and the butt of the company's rough jokes, while on guard had suddenly shouted "Aux armes!" and let go with his rifle. Every one had risen to the walls, the Véry flares had gone up, and in their glare we had seen a poor old village dog running away dragging a leg.

Now for a moment we thought something like this had happened. The men under their breaths began to make uncomplimentary remarks as to the ancestry of the gentleman who had awakened them. "Hell, there isn't going to be any fight," I thought. Just then I saw a flash in the darkness, and a bullet went buzzing over my head. And suddenly the whole night was winking with rifle flashes while flocks and squadrons of bullets went singing overhead, or with a cat's miauling ricocheted from our walls. A Véry light went up; in the glare we saw the slope above us, the level between, the ground on all sides, filled with silent charging forms, and let go with all we had. Simultaneously, as the light betrayed their secrecy, they broke out into a chorus of wildest yells.

We were shouting, too. A man in such a fight

shouts without knowing it. At first I was nervous. There is on the Lebel rifle a little button which must be slipped back when you are reloading. After letting go what I had in the magazine, which did not take long, I started to reload without remembering the little button. As fast as I would push a cartridge in, it would spring out. Finally I remembered, and simultaneously I must have gone mad with the ardor of the fight. I shot till my heated rifle burned my hands. I thought I was perfectly silent, yet I remember Lieutenant Vernon coming to me and advising me not to yell so loud. "You tell them where you are, when you do that," he pointed out judiciously.

It was terribly confusing fighting at first. Few Véry lights were yet going up, and the night was black. It was punctured by the stabbing flashes of their rifles, and at those flashes we shot. But a lot of them managed to rush by between the walled camps, and enter the village. The camp there, and the fortified état-major, held stanchly, but they penetrated the cavalry quarters. Twenty-nine Cossacks guarding them were butchered, and the horses of the squadron captured.

It was one thing, however, to capture the

horses and another to get them out. When these wild tribesmen, on the captured horses, began to gallop out of the village, a slight greenness of dawn was in the air. We could see better. Also a horse is bigger than a man, easier to see and easier to shoot at. We turned our fire upon the horses, just visible in the growing light. They were our own horses, but we did not think of that. We would bring down a horse, and then get the rider, dismounted and helpless between our enfilading fires. Few of these got out alive, though meanwhile their brothers on the slope above poured their fire down upon us.

It was now almost daylight, and now came a lull. In our little redoubt the best marksmen were held to the *créneaux*, exchanging shots with the snipers, while the rest of us sat down against the wall and rested. And some of us *bleus* thought that the affair was over. As a matter of fact, this had been simply a preliminary skirmish, a first maneuver, which had more than partly succeeded, in that they had dismounted us and left us without cavalry.

In a few minutes, just as the day was definitely breaking, again came the cry "Aux armes!" and we all sprang to our loopholes.

The sight that now met us was an extraordinary one, and one that might have been terrifying had we not been by this time mad with the lust of the fight. Down the slope at the bottom of the hill, the Druses were pouring down upon us as if it were the very earth itself moving in landslide —five thousand of them on horse and foot. The infantry was ahead; right behind was the cavalry, ready to charge through the infantry's opening ranks to take the lead at the first break. They were all in light fighting equipment, without their burnous, in their short jackets, their colored head-dresses flapping. They brandished their weapons and howled as they came, and at their head were four great black banners flanking the emir.

For a moment I thought I was dreaming. For riding ahead between their black banners was their emir, on his beautiful blooded stallion, and he wore a medieval suit of chain armor, and one of those helmets with flaps of chain mail such as you see in museums—a suit used perhaps hundreds of years ago against the Frankish crusaders.

Our machine-guns were chattering, our rifles were cracking, but this mass of men was coming along seemingly unimpeded. Coming in fanatical charge, a moving carpet over the earth, yelling like fiends, their "Ya Illah Lah, Ya Illah Lah, Ya Illah Lah."

They were attacking all of the camps, but to us it seemed as though it was at us and our little fort and its sixty or seventy men that these fanatic thousands were sweeping. Not so fanatical, either, as not to be plentifully armed with good rifles, using good ammunition, and a plentiful supply of German potato-masher grenades.

In a minute the thing was like a football game, a constant rush upon us with no time to breathe. Time and time again the fringe of the charge died within a few feet of the walls. I fired till my rifle was hot and steamed in my hands. Then I threw grenades. Then I fired again.

In between, I had the time to catch a glimpse of a strange and rather magnificent sight. The first rush, though it had overwhelmed none of the camps, had carried the attackers headlong into the village, which was to our right. Near the center of the village, but on our side of it, was a mound that gave a point of vantage. In a rush like that of a wave up the slope of a beach, the emir topped this mound with his four great black banners. He threw his horse upon its haunches, pivoted it till he faced us, and simultaneously his color guard planted the banners on the mound, sticking them into the soil with great strokes, as though they meant them to stay there forever. Dismounting calmly under the flapping ensigns, he set himself to directing the fighting from there. Suddenly all the flat roofs of the village were alive with snipers who poured a fire into our camp which we could not answer, busy as we were with the charges down there.

They were still coming, wave upon wave. The slope down which they descended and which added to their impetus, was dotted with great stones and cut up with little walls which gave them some shelter till they had debouched upon the plain for their last dash into the open. They came down that slope, flowing from stone to stone, from wall to wall like a great cataract of water; then they'd rush the last space, and in the face of our withering fire almost reach our wall. Some, as a matter of fact, died in its very shadow. When everything was over we found the body of one of those wild dervishes with both hands upon the wall. He had seemingly charged our machine-guns with bare hands. There he lay, his twisted fingers clutching the inside corner of the parapet, the brains of his burst cranium scattered over it, and curiously we counted thirty distinct bullet-holes in his twisted body.

This was later, of course. We were not counting anything now, not giving any heed to the dead. The living held all of our attention. They kept coming; every moment we seemed on the point of being overwhelmed; our small redoubt —a mere circular stone wall, breast high and hastily thrown up yesterday, and holding at most some seventy men—was like a little boat tossed in a tremendous sea. We'd fire with our rifles till they got too close, then, stooping and rising, picked up the grenades lying about our feet and let them have them in the face. During rare short lulls, they'd be sniping from behind rocks and low stone walls—one of which was not more than sixty feet away from us. Then we'd snap to our rifle barrels the *tromblon*-like attachment for the rifle grenades, and dislodge them from behind their shelter with tremendous explosions that sometimes sent arms and legs up in the air together with the rock and the sand. The din was terrific. Our two machine-guns kept up a continuous rattling, rifles cracked, ricocheted bullets screeched like cats, the grenades exploded with big booms, and yells were always in the air. "Ya Illa Lah, Ya Illa Lah, Ya Illah Lah." They filled the air with this rhythmic cry, and then long streams of unintelligible Arab which were threats of what they were going to do to us Christian dogs. And we, in turn, roared curses in several languages and defiantly called them to come on and be Illa-lahed.

Little by little we settled down to calm, sure work. I did not know I had been shouting till my lieutenant told me. I caught a flash of Sylvestre Budney, my fellow *bleu*, firing calmly from the angle of one of the bastion entrances, a cigarette in his mouth. I put one in mine. Afterward there was always a cigarette in my mouth, often a dead butt, it is true—but at that I managed to get away with six packs during the day, and all my comrades fought smoking.

Time and time again the situation seemed utterly desperate. So far we had saved our little fort, but we had not been able to keep the hordes from filtrating in between into the village, and the village was now full of them. From its flat roofs their snipers fired directly into our camp, and altogether taken up with the rushes from the plain and the slope, we could not attend to them.

Out of its narrow alleys, massed attacks kept pouring toward us, mingling with the charges from down the hill; we were busy indeed. Our rifles heated, we threw grenades while they cooled.

Each attack, when broken by our fire, would vanish behind the stones and walls during a recess filled with ardent sniping. Then, rested, reëncouraged, reëxhorted by their leaders, they'd come again with renewed fury. And thus hour after hour after hour. In the village we could hear what was left of the cavalry squadron stoutly defending their houses; and that fortified house of the état-major and headquarters company was spitting fire from over all its holes. But several times such a tumult and a shouting arose over there, that we thought the état-major—our commandant and his staff—had been overwhelmed and butchered. We could see now and then the other little camps resisting like ours—little boats they looked like, rocking in a great sea. But most of the time we did not see anything but that which was close at hand—and several times to me, and the others also, those were wild rolling eyeballs capsizing in the death throes just in time. It was some time before I realized what was really happening. At first I thought I was shooting badly; then little by little I saw that with several bullets in them, these fanatic tribesmen came on, to die on our barbed wire. And the wounded kept on fighting. Bleeding to death, from behind a stone, or even in the open, they kept firing till the last convulsive twitch. Now and then, in the midst of that massed fighting, you'd get hypnotized into some private combat of your own. There was a special Druse, I remember, whom it took me a long time and extraordinary pains to kill. He was mounted on one of our stolen horses, and riding stretched low along the mane like an Indian. I did not seem to be able to hit him. I shot and shot, and apparently kept missing him. Finally I aimed at the horse and brought it down. But the Druse appeared to be still unhurt, and holding his rifle started to crawl rapidly for cover. My bullets raised little spurts of sand all about him—I did not seem to be able to hit him. But his crawling slowed and slowed: I *was* hitting him. Slowly, though, he crawled on, and finally vanished behind a rock—and immediately a bullet went whining by, not an inch from my head. From behind his rock he kept sniping at me. I put on the grenade attachment on my rifle and sent several of the big grenades over there. The third one struck right behind the rock. There was a tremendous boom, a little volcano of sand and smoke rose into the air, and I knew I had got my Druse at last.

There was another moment I remember in which I seemed hypnotized as if in a dream. From one of the stone hedges not more than a hundred feet away, a little detachment of about ten Druses suddenly appeared in a headlong, screeching charge for my part of the wall. And what almost paralyzed me was that they were all withered old men with long ragged beards that fell lower than their waists and almost to their knees. Into our concentrated fire these queer old gnomes came and seemed to bear a charmed life. I fired and fired, and it was having no more effect than if they had been air. While the concentrated fire from my right and my left seemed as impotent. They reached our piteous little strand of barbed wire—all we had been able to put up on our arrival the day before—all together started to step over, their knees parting their long beards—and then abruptly, all together in one movement, all collapsed. They had been carrying bullets in them almost from their first appearance from behind the wall; I'll wager that several had been dead on their feet as they charged. They lay there in a heap, the last squirmings of which we stilled with our grenades.

So intent, of course, was our attention on the outside, that we had little time to know or notice what was happening inside our hard-pressed walls. I remember our Lieutenant Vernon clearly, though, slim and stoop-shouldered, his face bristling with several days' beard, walking about coolly, standing up, disdaining to take cover, one hand in his pocket, the other holding a huge automatic pistol. He'd come and stand behind you, and point out special men to shoot at, and when you succeeded, would give you a little pat on the shoulder and say, in the tone of one who has just had a good drink, "Ça, that was a good shot." Then he'd move on to another man. In between he'd step over to the wall and do a little sharpshooting himself with his automatic. The *adjudant-chef* was walking about in the same way, quietly directing the men's fire at the worst points and the most troublesome snipers. He had a preference for grenades, however; instead of an automatic he carried a handful of these which he would fling himself when things got at the warmest and we seemed about to be definitely rushed, or merely as a pastime between little talks with the men. The *infirmier* or first aid man—we had just one—had made himself a first aid station by digging a hole in the center of the camp, amid the boxes. But he was not there often, nor long. He would go across the bullet-swept space to the wounded, take them or drag them into his hole, put on the dressing, then, seizing his rifle, with a yell would be with us at the wall, an angel of mercy one moment, an enthusiastic killer the next. The machine-gun crews were firing without a let-up and severely suffering from the snipers, who concentrated upon them. There was another man who had volunteered for a dangerous job. He was a Pole, named Esquisert (I think he's in the United States now). From the ammunition dump at the center of the camp, he would fill his *musette* with grenades and crawling across the exposed ground would reach the wall. This he would circle, passing, of course, exposed places, distributing the grenades. Once when he passed me, I stole the whole full *musette* from him. He started to wrestle it back from me. I held on, and suddenly he quit and said like a school boy, "If you don't give me back my grenades, I'll tell the lieutenant." I didn't give them back; I was busy using them by this time; and I never did learn whether he told the lieutenant on me and got me some secret black mark!

All this time I had been fighting with an Italian named Morgardi to my left, and a bugler, named Pohl, a German, to my right, each of us holding about fifteen feet of wall. I think we had been fighting thus for about an hour, and just at the time a sergeant named Rath was standing behind us, directing our fire, when in a new rush a Druse grenade, a potato-masher from Germany, struck squarely on the parapet among us.

I saw Morgardi enveloped in a cloud of black smoke; he gave a yell, put his hands to his eyes, and crumpled to the ground, dead, the whole top of his head torn away, and the inside showing. Sergeant Rath sank to the ground, and started to crawl away, covered with blood and desperately wounded. Pohl, to my right, was bleeding from a wound in the head, but still groggily sticking to his post.

My rifle had been torn out of my hands in the

concussion. I stepped over and picked it up, and found that the whole butt had been blown away. I was unhurt. The man to my left had been killed, the one to my right wounded, the one behind me desperately wounded, my gun had been wrecked, and I had not been touched. I picked up Morgardi's rifle, and kept on shooting, my part of the wall being now much extended.

For a little while bugler Pohl stubbornly carried on. But the blood flowing down his head was blinding him; he could not see, and the *infirmier*, having placed Rath under shelter in his hole at the center of the camp, now led the bugler away, protesting and resisting. I then took his rifle, which was the best in the section; an almost new gun which he treated like a watch, and kept always in perfect order. And in all that stress, I was for a minute like a child with a new toy.

After Morgardi and Pohl were gone, I worked with a little Parisian named Fleury who had been farther to the left. We two were now responsible for a space which had been guarded by four men. We kept moving from loophole to loophole to disconcert the snipers, and soon fell into excellent team work. He was a little fellow from Montmartre, no bigger than a minute, short, thick-set; he fought in continuous hot temper, eyes popping out of his head, mustache bristling, active as a squirrel and tireless—a marvelous fighter. He was a dead shot with the rifle, and of uncanny skill with the grenade, and quick as lightning in all his movements. Slarski, a Pole who had been wounded and could no longer stand up and shoot, volunteered to stay with us. Remaining on the ground he would pass us our ammunition and grenades as we needed them and we three made a fine team.

It was then I revised an opinion I had been forming about the hard-boiled old Legionaires of our outfit. I found that these rascally nuisances of peace days, always drunk, always quarreling, always late at *appel* and in continuous hot water, were transformed when real work began. Watching them, I could hardly believe the change. It was not only that they were brave, fighting with utmost heroism. But they were patient and enduring, full of devotion and self-sacrifice, helpful to every one, and obeying every order not only without a murmur but with a sort of self-immolating alacrity. They were lions to the enemy, lambs to their officers and comrades. I never cared much what they did after that.

Also I was learning of the difference in national temperaments when under fighting conditions. The French, like my little Parisian, were full of fire and élan, fought worked up to a high pitch of emotional excitement under which they were cool as steel; the Germans were stolid and quiet, but held to their rifles and everything else like grim death, immensely stubborn. And the Russians were fatalists, not caring whether they were going to die or not. As for the American temperament—I was too busy to watch it.

But other things were happening. Simon, our *adjudant-chef*, had been shot in the arm. Disdainful of his wound, he was still calmly walking about directing us; but since he could no longer throw grenades, he had secured a light carbine with which he amused himself now and then, shooting with his left arm. Sergeant Fischer, a German, had been shot through the head; and we were obliged to see him dying for a long time, his mouth opening and closing like that of a fish laid out on hot sand. Another sergeant, Sergeant Krierisch, a big German, had been wounded in such a way as to give for a long time a subject for our section's rough wits. He was standing at the parapet, shouting out an order, when a bullet, coming from the Druse, slapped into his open mouth, coming out through the right cheek, and there he stood, cursing fearfully, spitting out blood, teeth and splinters of jaw-bone, refusing the *infirmier's* aid, shaking his fist at the foe and insisting on fighting on. It took three men to get him off to the infirmary. And later he was to be joshed often over this day when, opening his mouth wide to bawl an order, he had swallowed a bullet.

Pitiful things were happening too. One of the men, shot in the chest, lay dying all day in the sand. He had been sent over from another section just before the attack, and we did not know who he was. Time and time again, when we thought him dead, one or the other of us would notice that he seemed to be murmuring. Some one would crawl to him across the zone of fire to see what he wanted. It was always water. "De l'eau, de l'eau," he murmured. We had very little water; we were in fact dying with thirst. But always some one would give a little out of his canteen, prop him up maybe a bit, then crawl back across the zone of fire. This kept up all day. He was slowly bleeding to death internally, but each time we thought him finally dead we'd see his lips begin to work, and finally some one would simply have to crawl over, and it was always the same thing, "de l'eau, de l'eau." He did this all day; it took him twelve hours to die.

Somewhere about nine or ten o'clock (we had been fighting since three in the morning) the enemy, broken by our fire, let up. There was a lull. The massed rushes ceased and the Druses contented themselves with firing from behind rocks, walls and from the roofs of the village.

While our best shots were kept at the wall, the rest of us slumped down along the bottom and rested. We were of course terribly weary, and stripped to the waist, looked like pirates. We had been cut off from water, the well being on the other side of the village, and of course unreachable; we had very little in our *bidons*, and were almost mad with the thirst. Lieutenant Vernon got out some of the meager supplies (they were in boxes which served as shelter to the *infirmier's* improvised first aid station) and carefully distributed them. One tin of *singe* was given to each four men to be shared. Herschkorn, a little

Frenchman, volunteered to get wine. With a canvas bucket in each hand, he crawled under the snipers' fire to where the barrel was kept, and crawled back with the pails almost full. Each man was given a *quart*, a quarter of a liter, which we consumed immediately.

Meanwhile our best shots at the wall were giving some attention to the snipers who, in the press of the charges, had been all too neglected. These sharpshooters were Herschkorn, a Frenchman; Brix, an Austrian, who was to be killed later at Rezzas; Costanovitch, a long, lank Russian; Bolse, an Alsatian; a little German called Kupe; and Fleury, the little Parisian from Montmartre who had fought with me. They were all veterans with five or ten years of service, who took great pride in their shooting. They did not waste ammunition. When they shot, it was because they saw something. When they shot at something, they hit it. When they hit, they killed.

I joined them as soon as I had eaten, and we tried to pick off the snipers on the flat roofs of the village. These, constantly in movement, in view only when leaping from one roof to the other, were hard to pick, but every now and then one of my comrades succeeded, and we could see the little body, made small by distance, pitch off the roof like a doll, or sprawl with arms over the edge for all the world like a puppet at a *guignol.*

Then some one said, let's get the emir. His horse had been led away, but he was still standing there on the mound in the village, surrounded by his guard, the big black banners flapping above him. I suppose it is not etiquette for an emir's guard of honor to seek cover, or God knows what strange contempt of us and of death, or what trust in charms, or what fanaticism held them there. But with that little Parisian and Costanovitch and Herschkorn and our other sharpshooters shooting close, and the rest of us doing as well as we could, they began to drop one after the other on the mound. Still they remained, the emir, in his chain armor and casque, as still as a piece in a museum. Then finally we got him. He was standing one moment, he was down the next, and there was nothing on the mound but sprawling bodies and the upright flapping black banners.

The situation suddenly became more grave. Lieutenant Vernon had been taking stock of the munitions, and now he sent out orders that we must shoot less freely, that we must husband our cartridges. He strolled among us himself. "Be very sparing," he said. "Be avaricious. Don't waste. Shoot only when you can kill. When they rush, wait till they are close. We haven't much ammunition left."

Cheerful news, with the Druses now beginning to move forward again in renewed attack! But now there was heard a roaring in the air and looking up we saw seven or eight airplanes in the sky. They dropped bombs on the Druses; they came down low and raked them with machine-gun fire. This was more spectacular than effective, we knew. The Druses, hugging close their rocks and stone hedges, merely arched their backs like cats in the rain. But then the planes, circling and dropping still lower, passed over our camps as we yelled like mad and waved our kepis at them. And as they slowly vanished in the distance, winging back toward Ghazalé, we knew that they had reconnoitred well, that they had seen our peril and our plight, and in a few minutes would be reporting it at headquarters. Reinforcements would be rushed from Ghazalé. We made calculations. Twenty kilometers' marching from Ghazalé; the relief should be here by four. Four! That seemed a long time away.

We saw now that our fate depended upon a race between the relief and the steady draining of our depleted ammunition store.

Then the new attack was on, and we figured no longer.

Whoever was the strategist behind that hill which faced us, who threw the Druses forward that day, had a flexible mind that learned from experience. That first terrible assault at dawn had been by men coming down in dense masses in which our fire had done terrific execution. The mode of attack now had been changed.

The long slope, between our camp and the mountain, down which they charged, was all cut up with low stone hedges that separated fields, and made corrals in peace times for the sheep of the villagers. As the Druses came down this slope now in renewed attack, they were making use of every bit of the cover. In extended order, in small detachments, they'd rush behind a hedge, fire for a while from there, then rush or crawl to another. Thus, almost invisible, these thousands were advancing upon us like a subterranean river.

We were reserving our fire, mindful of the

orders and feeling of the situation. We were firing very slowly and carefully; most of the time all we saw was a bounding form going through the air from one rock to the other. My little Parisian, still fighting to my left—and now we had a lot of wall to hold—now and then caught one of these out of the air; but most of us were reserving our fire for closer quarters.

There was at the bottom of the slope a last space that must be rushed to get at us. Whenever they reached this, we suddenly became prodigal and let go with everything we had; at that, they sometimes died on our barbed-wire strand, and sometimes almost at the wall. It was then my little Parisian was at his best. He was good with his rifle, but with grenades absolutely uncanny. He could almost throw them around corners. Failing to reach home, the remnants of the charging Druses would retreat behind the nearest walls; and my Parisian, lobbing carefully, would dislodge them with grenades landing on their backs. "Ça y'est," he'd say each time, "Ça y'est!"

We also had to give attention, when not too hard pressed from ahead, to the snipers on the roofs of the village, which was to our right. From their elevation they could pour their fire right into our camp; we could not get away from it; while from the attackers on the ground we had the protection of our walls as we shot snugly out of our *créneaux*, the danger on that side being of a rush that would finally crush in our little redoubt and overwhelm us.

Thus the hours passed, wearily, in constant fighting, heat, clamor, death and blood, and our ammunition ebbed. We began to ask each other the time. Finally it was four o'clock, the hour we had fixed in our minds as that of the relief. But there came no relief. Nothing changed. The Druses were still firing without let-up. We were still in Hell. Half past four. The men began to curse bitterly. Would that relief never come? The lieutenant, with his binoculars, looked anxiously toward Ghazalé. A new attack debouched out of the village, and we stopped that. The wounded Druses dotting the ground kept firing; we would have to finish them one by one, shooting carefully, wasting not a shot. But still the store kept getting lower and lower to the constant leakage. The lieutenant was raising his binoculars more and more often toward Ghazalé, but from Ghazalé nothing was coming.

It was now well past four o'clock, and no

relief. The lieutenant took a last count of the munitions, a last long look out of his binoculars, then told us to stick our bayonets into the ground.

Each man pulled his bayonet out of its sheath and stuck it into the ground by his side, to have it ready to fix when came the last command, for the final act would come. The lieutenant brought out the last of the munitions and it was passed around. The machine-gun men had all been put out of action by the snipers; we tore the last of their ammunition belts and passed around the cartridges. When the distribution had been finished, I had about twenty-five cartridges left. Some of the men had less than half of that. A few grenades were at the feet of each man. And by his side, sticking in the ground, was his bayonet, ready to be fixed when, at the last, the enemy would be within and the final cutthroating begun. A word went around the wall, passed from man to man. "Keep a last cartridge for yourself." All the old Legionaires had fought in Morocco and had seen their wounded tortured. They were not sure if it would be the same with the Druses, but they were going to take no chances.

The Druses seemed to have sensed our extremity, and were getting together for a final assault. The streets of the village were packed with them, chanting, singing, working themselves up to a frenzy under the exhortations of their leaders. Behind the stone walls on the slope the same movements were occurring. The marabouts went from detachment to detachment, yells were rising everywhere. Then the cavalry, massed behind the infantry, almost at the top of the crest, which had been waiting all day for its time, formed in long lines, and began to descend slowly.

Meanwhile we had ceased to answer their fire at all. With just a few watchers at the *créneaux* to call us when the final rush began, we sat at the foot of the wall, fanned ourselves with our kepis, and refused to shoot no matter how much they shot, or tried to provoke us into shooting. Backs to the wall, out of sight, fanning ourselves, we acted as though they did not exist, refusing to shoot, holding on to our precious munitions, and promising ourselves a warm last quarter of an hour.

It was perhaps this inertia, this silence of ours which, through the suspicion it engendered, the fear of some trap, delayed their *coup de grâce*. There is no doubt that if they had charged at this instant, we could not have held them. The cavalry, leaping the low wall, would have been among us like a tornado, and it would have been the end. But they delayed, their horsemen walking slowly into striking position, the infantry still inflaming itself with its chants and its clamor.

And then, as we sat there, fanning ourselves, suddenly we pricked our ears and looked at each other.

Behind us, on the side opposite the slope down which had come the attacks, the ground rose in another long slope to a crest. And from behind that crest, far off, there came to our ears a tiny brassy sound, a tiny brassy music, as if from the insides of a closed victrola. Brass bugles, far over there. And they were sounding tinily the precipitated, alert, stirring call of the charge, "En avant."

The tiny sound was swelling and growing clear. It leaped out of the victrola and became real. It was swelling, nearing. We sprang to our feet with a shout. Behind that crest over there, still far but fast nearing, massed bugles were singing over and over again, "En avant! En avant! En avant! En avant!"

Then rifle fire broke out over there and the rattling of machine-guns. Druse cavalry came running by. Suddenly with a long hiss, a forty-five millimeter shell lit in the center of our camp. It exploded without hitting any of us and we actually welcomed it with a roar of laughter. "They must think we are dead, those over there," we growled. Now more shells began to rain about as some invisible battery found its range.

Meanwhile the massed bugles behind that crest somewhere were raising and raising their cry. "En avant! En avant! En avant! En avant!" Clearer and clearer, louder and louder, nearer and nearer the sound came. "En avant! En avant! En avant! En avant!"

And suddenly over the crest came pouring in extended line the Sixteenth Regiment of Algerian Tirailleurs, which had come by forced marches from Ghazalé to our rescue. Down they swept upon the Druses. Behind them came the massed bugles, singing still, hysterically, "En avant! En avant! En avant! En avant!"

Down they swept in beautiful extended order, rising and falling, rising and falling. And as they charged they were yelling like the Druses, their call upon Allah. But the Allah they invoked was a French Allah well supplied with reserves, with discipline and machine-guns, while the poor Druses by now were calling upon a discouraged and empty-handed Allah. Down the slope the Tirailleurs swept, and filled the plain. Those in line with the village poured into it and began a house-to-house slaughter; the others swept on to the right and the left of it, up the slopes down which the Druses had charged and up which they were now fleeing.

First letting go the last of our preciously husbanded ammunition in a general wild discharge after the disappearing fugitives, we opened the gates of our redoubt and strolled out with hands in our pockets.

CHAPTER VIII

THE Druses, in retreating before the Tirailleurs, had left a rear guard which fought stubbornly. That part of it, in fact, which was cut off in the village, resisted for hours in sanguinary house-to-house fighting. When night came the Trailleurs were still at it, forcing their way little by little from house to house. We could hear the shooting, the yells, and easily imagined what was going on in this hand-to-hand work in which neither side was giving quarter.

By night-time, we had been revictualled, watered and re-ammunitioned and our camp had resumed its regular military routine. Standing guard that night had a tragic character. Every now and then a detached shot in the village, a cry, told us that the terrible but forced work of extermination was going on over there in the darkness. And every now and then something like a ghost would flit by. It would be some Druse who had got out and was trying to reach his people. He would have no chance. From our camp, from the others, shots stabbed the night, and the ghost melted, became less than ghost.

Outside of standing guard, we slept, heavily, the sleep of utter exhaustion. The rising sun, though, brought no vacation. We found that after a battle there is still work to do. I noticed, however, that some of the old Legionaires woke with an air of anticipation. Their nostrils twitched as though they were smelling something pleasant. I learned later what it was which thus tickled their nostrils. It was the chance of there being loot. After a battle there is work to do; but if it has been a decent battle, there is also loot.

We looked of course like scarecrows. Our eyes were bloodshot and half shut; we were caked with dirt and blood, our uniforms were in rags. But there was yet not time to primp up, nor the means, our rations of water, what with the new-comers, being shorter than ever. The different *corvées* were allotted and I was one of those named for the *corvée* of the dead. This meant our own dead, within our camp.

So I went through the clothes of those of our men who had died fighting with us that night. We searched their pockets, gathering together all their poor trinkets, their knives, their pipes, their papers; we went through their packs doing the same thing. We made little bundles of these objects, to go to the proper office, and from there to their families together with the notice of their deaths—a terrible and gruesome job in the heat. This done, the bodies were placed on trucks to be taken back to the cemetery at Ghazalé.

After that I was put on a *corvée* of *ravitaillement*, and worked like a stevedore bringing in meat, potatoes, onions and beans! The fact that I was taller and bigger than the average Legionaire often drew upon me this unpleasant labor, and any, in fact, in which a man carried a load! On this day, however, the *corvée* took me about and gave me a chance to see—and I made it last as long as possible and take me over as much ground as possible.

The first thing that struck the eye was the number of Druse dead. They lay scattered over the open places, but behind each wall, or shelter, they lay piled like snow drifted by the wind. It seemed almost incredible even as you looked. Every now and then some soldier wandering about gave a shout, and you ran over to a new wall and found a new heap of them.

In the village there was going on a great to-do as, to the orders of their colonel, the Tirailleurs of the Eighteenth, our rescuers, cleaned it out. Colonel Andrea had ordered that all the dead bodies should be spread out in line in front of the village to serve as an example, for this was a village "soumis," which had accepted French authority and paid taxes, and then had proved treacherous. The Titrailleurs were using Druse prisoners to help them, or, in fact, to do the heaviest of the job. Bodies were being taken down from roofs, brought up from cellars, and dragged through the street to be placed in the gruesome file. At the same time the bodies of the Cossack Legionaires who had been surprised and overwhelmed in the first attack were being moved out, to be taken on trucks to Ghazalé. And the horses which had died in the stables or in the streets were being dragged out of the village, to join the line of human cadavers.

As I say, this work was being done by Druse prisoners under the guard of the Tirailleurs. Later we were to hear volleys in the village. The Druse prisoners, having finished their work, were being executed by firing squads, on order of the colonel of the Tirailleurs. I was told later that every one of these prisoners had been shot.

In explanation of this, I can only say that the village having been a village "soumis," that is, claiming to be friendly, the attack was to be considered as a treacherous one. And also that the Druses in combat never gave quarter nor expected it, their wounded firing or using their knives to the last. The captives had expected nothing less and met their death stoically, without flinching or asking sympathy.

I was to be the witness of another terrible drama, the act of a semi-crazed soldier. This was a German, a machine-gunner of the 15th Company. He had lost his *copain*, his "buddy" who had been killed during the fighting of the night; all the morning he had been brooding about it. When noon came he filled a *bidon* with water, loaded his revolver and set out on a tour of the battle-field. There were still among the Druse dead some who were only wounded. The mad trooper would find one of these, go to him with all the marks of compassion and pity, raise him on his knee, and proffer his *bidon* of water. Then just as the wounded man, delirious with thirst, avidly clutched the bottle, he would blow out his brains with a shot of his revolver.

He had been going about for quite a while before any one noticed what he was doing, and a horrified sergeant started after him, calling on him to stop. It took more than the sergeant to bring him back, however. It took an entire squad, and the man was foaming at the mouth at being deprived of his vengeance—the avenging of his *copain*.

Meanwhile some of my comrades too had not been idle. Old campaigners that they were, they had cannily got themselves into the activity which was most popular at such a time and promising of most amusement—and result. One of the things always done after a battle such as this was to gather up the weapons of the dead enemy, which otherwise would have served again in the hands of live ones.

But going about among the dead to gather up their rifles, one must also be sure not to leave behind any minor weapons such as pistols, or daggers, or even knives—which means one must go through the pockets of the dead. And there, now and then, if one is lucky, one finds other things. Hence the popularity of this special *corvée* among the old reprobates who filled my section. After a time they began to straggle back into camp laden with loot—incrusted daggers, sabers, silver spangles, watches—and money—which they showed off to each other—pleased as children. Delaporte, my friend of the *bidons*, who at Ghazalé had so handily got me out of my difficulties, had been the luckiest, though Herschkorn and Bolse also had done well, and Sylvestre Budney, the *bleu*, not so badly for a debutante. Delaporte had actually come across some one's hidden treasure in a cellar of the village—coins mixed with trinkets and jewelry to the tune of nearly five thousand francs. For months afterward, whenever he was where it could be done, he was to get gloriously drunk till the result of his frugal morning's labor at last was dissipated.

But it was Fleury, my little Parisian friend, who had fought by my side along the wall in the night, who had the real success. Characteristically enough he had gone off on this job with an eye rather to glory than to material success. In the afternoon he came staggering back. He was laden like a camel with knives and sabers, he dragged six rifles along the ground, and he bore the late emir's banners—the big black banners under the shadow of which we had fought.

This pleased Lieutenant Vernon mightily, and he rewarded the little Frenchman with a half-*bidon* of wine. He had just finished consuming this reward and was a bit flushed and unsteady, when Colonel Andrea, commandant of the Sixteenth Tirailleurs which had relieved us, came into camp on a little visit. Full of the ingenuous courage which wine gives a simple nature, Fleury immediately picked up his banners and walked over to the colonel. "*Bonjour, mon colonel*," he said, "tutoying" him familiarly. "*Regarde-moi ça, mon colonel; ne sont-ils pas chics mes drapeaux?* Look here what I've got. Aren't they chic, my flags?" The colonel smiled. "*Ah oui, ils sont chics*," he answered, "*et tu es un bon soldat.*" He turned to us all, "*Bonjour, mes Legionaires, comment ça va-t-il?*" "*Ca va très bien*," the little Parisian answered for us all. "*Et tu sais*—thou knowest—if you want any more done, just call on us!" The colonel smiled, then snapped to rigid position, gave us the homage of a formal salute and went on, smiling to himself.

That night we really slept. The night before had been a wild one, full of noise and alarms, with the sentries of the Tirailleurs shooting at every shadow. This one proved comparatively quiet and we slept like logs.

We woke to find ourselves the heroes of the camp. Reinforcements were arriving constantly and digging in, some sort of a big movement was being prepared. Long lines of trucks, pieces of artillery, camel convoys kept coming upon the plain, troops of all kinds—spahis, tirailleurs, chasseurs, Senegalese, the Battalion of Syria, *Partisans*—irregular Syrian cavalry, and even cavalry of Russian Mohammedan *Tcherkesh*, wearing their round fur caps. There were two batteries of seventy-fives—Metropolitan troops from France—and a mountain battery served by Malagasy from Madagascar.

Among all these troops we swaggered, filthy, unwashed, unshaven, the seats of our pants out, covered with an amalgam of dust, sweat and blood, the kepi down over one eye. Colonels and generals came to see us: we were the show of the camp. Camel trains from wells ten kilometers out had brought in water and filled the big concrete tank near the village, but what with the new arrivals, water was as scarce as ever and our allowance was still the meager one under which we had fought. We were not for wasting it, and went still unwashed, taking, I see it now, no little pleasure in our formidable appearance. Boys fresh from France, *bleus* from the artillery detachments, came to see us. They looked at us with big eyes, and we filled them with terrible tales, and sold them souvenirs. They were all crazy for souvenirs and some had money. We'd sell them an old saber for seventy francs, a dagger for twenty; the looters of my section were getting rich.

That does not mean we were idle. We still had our *corvées*, and mine was still that of *ravitaillement.* A dump of provisions had been established at the *état-major*, in the village, about a quarter of a mile from the camp, and from there I was carrying on my back sacks of coffee or beans, or rolling barrels of wine.

Our regular *caporal d'ordinaire* in charge of such a detail had been wounded and evacuated to a hospital, and we had a new one who did not know his business well—which resulted in an unusual bit of good luck for us that night.

There was in our camp a big *tune*—a barrel

much larger than the usual kind we used—big around and as high as your chin. The new *caporal d'ordinaire* struck it a few blows with the knuckle of the hand, tipped it, listened, and pronounced it empty. Empty, it was simply in the way, so our squad was ordered to take it out of camp, and to the stores at the *état major* in the village, together with another empty barrel.

So we started, rolling our barrels across the ground, toward the village. We had gone only a little way, when the fellows with the big barrel, who had gotten ahead, suddenly stopped, put their ears to it, and then began to signal me wildly to come on. Kicking my barrel before me on the run, I soon reached them and heard the news. There was still wine in the big *tune*. I sought confirmation and shook it to and fro. Sure enough, if you put your ear up to it, you heard a pleasant swash and gurgle.

Near us was a little bank. Pushing all together we rolled the big barrel up there, and steadied it with stones at the proper angle and tapped it.

The size and force of the generous red stream that rewarded our ingenuity took us by surprise. Mouths up against it filled immediately, and noses too; in a second we were backing away all spattered, and the beautiful stream was pouring to the ground while we despairingly cursed. I happened to catch sight of an old oil-tin near by, seized it and placed it under. The others went scouting and found another; we sneaked to the camp and strolled back laden with *bidons* hurriedly and enthusiastically lent us.

When the barrel got to the *état-major* stores, it was really empty this time; it was we who were a little full. But we had not forgotten our comrades. The contents of the full *bidons*, of the oil-cans, were carefully distributed among the whole section that night, and at supper, each man found himself with an extra *quart*.

This, by the way, was to be our only celebration. We remained here for four days after the battle, which, remember, had taken place one day only after our arrival. The concentration of troops now going on about us meant something, we knew. On the fourth day we learned what it was, as the column started its march. We were going to the relief of Suweida, the high-perched post, besieged by the Druses, whose flash signals we had been seeing day and night.

We were glad to go. On the outside, our name was being extolled. The papers in Damascus had come out with long and enthusiastic accounts of our fight. General Sarrail had cited us "Order of the Army," the entire battalion in one citation, and our hard old Vingt-neuvième Compagnie de Marche separately in another. Meanwhile, ignoble, unwashed, we were living in a huge charnel pile. The heaps of Druse slain all over the plain, the gruesome exemplary line at the entrance of the village, the dead horses, all were uniting in making, to say it mildly, the air unfit to breathe.

I have been asked, Did you not bury the enemy dead? And I answer, We did not. One reason is, we couldn't. The warfare we were in —as all colonial warfare—was being conducted with forces so small in comparison to the results demanded, that it took all of our strength—and sometimes more than that—to take care of ourselves. We couldn't bury the enemy dead. When it was possible, they were burned by rear units coming after us. And the wounded? I have been asked. Well, we did not take care of the enemy wounded either. For the same reason: we couldn't. There were hardly enough ambulances for our own men. The Druses died where they fell, or in corners where they crawled, unattended.

Besides it was a war without quarter. Who had started it on those terms, I don't know, but firmly established on those terms it certainly was when I came into it. The Druse gave no quarter and wanted no quarter. The wounded Druse kept firing as long as he had ammunition; after that he stabbed at you with his knife; when he was too weak even to do that, he died—and we let him die. That is the way we fought, and looking back now, I think it was the only way to fight.

So we were glad to be leaving this huge charnel heap. The original inhabitants of the village—they had been in league with the enemy—had been ordered out of it forever. It was an empty and lugubrious place upon which we turned our backs as we marched away to the relief of Suweida.

CHAPTER IX

WHEN the column marched out of Mousseifré to the relief of Suweida, our battalion of Legionaires were placed as Guard of Convoy, and much was said about the rest we should get thus.

A column such as we were—the French call such a *groupe mobile*—marches across country in the following formation. The convoy, consisting of the tanks, the armored automobile, the camions, the ambulances, the artillery, the munitions, the supplies the *état-major*, or staff, is in the center and goes along the road. Ahead of it, deployed across the road and far to both sides, is a screen of cavalry. This is followed by the infantry, also deployed. Parallel to the course of the convoy to the right and the left march like screens—the outermost two of cavalry, the inner two of infantry. Behind the convoy comes more infantry, followed by a screen of cavalry. The convoy is thus in the center of a great protective square.

But on the flanks, inside the screens, and beside

the convoy, as further protection is the Guard of the Convoy. We were *Garde de Convoi* that day, on the left flank. This meant that we kept exact pace with the slow train, that while it went along the road, we tramped on the heights, up and down, up and down, and through the loose rocks of the open country at the side of the road. Also that we helped camions out of ruts, helped haul artillery pieces when stuck, made ourselves generally useful, in other words acted as guardians and godfathers to that great helpless innocent a convoy always proves itself to be. That was our rest, the reward for our labors of Mousseifré.

Our departure had been enlivened by a little incident. Our battalion had marched to the place where it was to take up the convoy, and we were waiting, *sac à terre*, for it to come along. Lined there along the road, dirty and infamous scarecrows, we were kidding the passing infantry, of other arms, in the way of the Legion, rudely and blasphemously alluding to what they were to expect ahead, and what the Druses would do to them, when down the road came a group of horsemen all bedecked in splendor. It was the general's staff, shined up and varnished. In the staff you don't wear khaki; you don't have to, you don't get shot at. And the general's staff was made up of officers of all arms so that in it were kepis of all colors, from the azure blue of the chasseurs, through the black of the engineers, to the scarlet red of the infantry. In the center was a kepi wreathed with golden oak leaves—that of General Gamelin himself. He had on a great horizon blue mantle with scarlet lining, thrown back over his shoulder; he and his staff, on their fine horses, were indeed a splendid sight. Along they came till opposite us scarecrows, and we all snapped to attention. He stopped. "*Bonjour, mes légionnaires,*" he said. "We attack Suweida to-morrow. *Allez-vous bien vous battre*—are you going to fight well?"

"*Toujours, mon colonel!*" we shouted back.

"*Alors, comme à Mousseifré*—then, just as at Mousseifré," he said, and with this subtle compliment left us, quite tickled with ourselves.

Finally the convoy came along, and we took up our march alongside. It was a fearfully hot day, and, keeping even with the convoy, when we were not down helping to extricate it, we marched over hills, down into dry water-courses, up out of them, across others, over loose rock, one of the most terrific marches I went through in my experience, and the memory of which still sticks. We had on, of course, our heaviest packs, and our water ration was most meager. Every other man carried a *bidon* of water and one of coffee, every other man, two *bidons* of water. This made three bidons of water and one of coffee to each four, but half of the water had to go to the kitchens.

We marched on thus all day, till afternoon, when we were up to the mountain called Tel Hadie, and then our cavalry bumped into the Druses who were holding the heights—and presto our "restful" occupation as convoy guard was over, and on the double-quick we were marched to the seat of trouble. The Druses from the top of the hill were firing at us. We dropped behind stones and fired back. They were higher than we were, and we could not get at them, and they had us pretty well flattened out behind our little screens of stone, and we could not well see how it would end. Then the blessed artillery was brought up. The seventy-fives came up the road, then up the slope, unlimbered and then proceeded to bump off the whole top of the hill. The low sun shone on it, an arid hill with no trees; I could see it clearly. Suddenly it became a volcano, spouting up earth, Druses and smoke.

This operation had taken about two hours and it was almost night. We dropped down, bedded the convoy down in a ravine, one of the dry water-courses of which this land is full, and occupied the crests around it. "Aux murailles!" The old cry. We built a wall, and then some brilliant higher-up decided we should move forward about two hundred yards. We built a second wall, but without much enthusiasm, and it was just enough to be called a wall. "What will you have for dinner, macaroni or rice?" called out the cook of my section. "Neither," we cried. "Let us have the water." We were cooks enough to know it took water to cook macaroni or rice. We preferred the water and went supperless to bed. We posted our sentinels and the night now became very cold, and suddenly the Druses started pouring volleys into us from the hill. We lay as we were, behind our low wall, and answered them, and after a while they got tired and we went to sleep at last.

Next morning we were up at three-thirty. We were now *flanc garde à gauche*, moving along to the left of the column. We debouched into a little valley—and there was Suweida before us. There was a little hill at the foot of the mountains, and right atop this hill was the citadel, with the village hanging on beneath to the hill's lower slope. The citadel, three stories with square bastions at the corners, looked very brave up there, with its little flag waving at the top.

The Druses made a last resistance, attacking our left flank, but we drove them off with machine-gun fire. And then, up through gardens, trees, and orchards, we went up into Suweida.

Our section camped in a big wheat-mill at one side of the town. I volunteered on the water detail, which took me to the citadel, and I went inside. All the openings were sand-bagged, loopholes were everywhere and beams reinforced the ceilings. There were gaping holes here and there, where the shells of the seventy-fives captured from the massacred Michaud column in August had been used by the Druses. I talked with some of the defenders. Cut off by the sudden revolt, they had been besieged for three months. They had had plenty of water, a well being in the courtyard, still had enough ammunition to last a year, but were low on food, their rations of late having consisted of biscuits. The Druses had kept them under constant fire, and when the captured seventy-fives had appeared, things had looked bad. But the Druses did not know how to manipulate the fuses of the shells, so that the shells, although making holes in the roofs and walls whenever they hit the citadel, did not explode. At that the garrison of three hundred had had seventy killed.

To my surprise I found that a woman was in the citadel. The wife of the commandant had been visiting him when the sudden revolt had broken out, and had been here throughout the siege. Later in the day I was to see her go by in an automobile, a young woman, dressed with Parisian chic, and looking as fresh as a daisy!

While I was thus getting the news, my water detail was stamping out there beyond the gates, held up by the press of the *corvées* of all the other outfits, all after the same thing—water from the big well in the middle of the citadel court. Many details were ahead of us, and horses and mules and camels. The lieutenant in charge of the guard at the gate spied us. "*En avant, la légion,*" he roared. "Come get your water first."

And passing all the other details, the prancing horses, the kicking mules, the biting camels, we went in first and filled our *bidons*. "You fellows have done the most fighting," said the lieutenant, "you'll get your water first."

This was on a Saturday, and next day was Sunday, blessed day of rest. It began with rifle inspection; our lieutenant, blear-eyed, unshaven, ragged, inspected us. Our rifles, our fighting accoutrement were clean—but we, no description would describe us. We still had not washed. Although the citadel well was plentiful and good, with the whole *groupe mobile* using it, there wasn't any to waste dashing it over one's head.

We lay around the rest of the day. Sunday is the day sacred to clothes-washing and sewing. But we had no water to wash with, and no thread. We worked a bit at our wall (of course we had got one up first thing upon our arrival), we lounged and slept.

At ten o'clock at night, I went up again to the citadel on the water detail. The press up there was worse than the first time, and the lieutenant at the gate was a new one, unimpressed by the Legion's late hardships. It took hours to get in through the swirl of tirailleurs and spahis and Senegalese, of camels, and mules, and rearing, fighting little Arabian stallions. Filling the *bidons* with a bucket let down at the end of a long rope took up more hours. It was two in the morning before we returned to our camp.

And at four the bugles got us up. Suweida was to be abandoned, the column was moving on, and the Legion was to act as rear guard.

Again we lined up, *sac à terre*, along the road, and hands in pockets, kepi over the right eye, watched the column march by, jesting the passing men, kidding them, using our bright wits. Lieutenant Vernon came in among us with cigarettes. "Well, Gilbert Clare, would you like a cigarette?" he asked in his careful English.

As a matter of fact, I had been without one since the night before. "Oh, yes, my lieutenant!"

And I took a big drag and was happy; it took little to make us happy in the Legion.

When the column had passed, the pioneers, of whom there are always two or three old ones in each section, went up into the village. The engineers during the night had mined Suweida's principal buildings. Our pioneers lit the long fuses, then came running back to us, and we set off, rear guard protecting the column from behind.

We had not marched far, deployed in battle formation, when behind us we heard a great roar and, turning, saw the citadel up in the air, then raining down in fragments. One after the other great explosions followed. The big mill where we had camped, the sultan's ex-palace, every building solid enough to be transformed into a stronghold was successively going up into the air and coming down as smoke, dust and shattered stone.

CHAPTER X

THE march back from the relief of Suweida proved a military promenade. After we had gone a distance in convoy formation, with the Legion as rear guard, General Gamelin decided there was no danger from the Druses for the time being; and the whole group marched along the road in column of threes as though we were in peace time. When this order came we were of course in the rear of the column, but we soon fixed that. Starting out on a forced march, taking to the rough ground along the road whenever necessary, we swung by outfit after outfit, throwing after each as we passed it, our rough Legion bits of wit, and came in first into Mousseifré.

Here, thank God, there was no wall to build. There stood our redoubt as we had left it. I am sorry to say it was not the only object still here as we had left it. The Druse dead were also still here, and the still more pestilential air.

But we were worn out; we slept. And the next morning were off early and still at full speed for Ghazalé, where we were to rest, re-form and reëquip.

When we had been here before, it had been a little lonely place; now we found it a great military camp, full of stores, troops and *matériel.* And also well supplied with canteens and everything that goes with them, all usual camp-followers. Syrians from Damascus, Greeks, had set up *bistros* in abandoned houses, where they sold bad cognac, worse *raké*, and still worse rum, together with all the *amer picon*, syrups, liqueurs and varied concoctions one sees in bottles white, yellow and green.

For a little while, everything went well. We had our first baths for weeks, we washed and shaved. We drew clean uniforms and washed our shirts, our socks, our underclothes, beating the dirt out of them with our hands against flat stones, in the primitive way, which we found a good way. We sewed, we were busy as housewives.

Then the hard birds of the Vingt-neuvième began to cut up in the way that is the way of the soldier of career in the monotony of peace days. They were drunk all the time, they missed *appel*, they defied their officers, these men whom I had seen in the fighting devotion itself, obedient as lambs, always ready to volunteer for the hardest dirtiest toil and the most dangerous service. They had Ghazalé in constant uproar, fighting with the Senegalese, the spahis, the tirailleurs, attacking the patrols. To pull one out of a canteen was an expedition. They reeled about in sodden fury, their mouths full of curses and threats, their knives always half out. They had drawn pay and had money. Some, like Delaporte, were rich with the looting at Mousseifré. And their only idea was to spend their money for drink, and drink whenever they had the chance.

Soon, many of them were in prison. The "prison" was a tent, but it was pitched between the wall (of course we had built a wall) and the thick barbed-wire entanglement. And one day, as prison guard, I had my first—shall I call it misunderstanding?—with my superiors.

The company that day was *compagnie du jour*. That is to say, it was serving the entire post with the different guards and patrols needed. My section was all out, and the little fiery red-headed Turkish sergeant had put me on guard over the tent holding the prisoners.

Guard duty is supposed to last two hours.

I had gone on at six in the morning. Eight o'clock came, and no relief. I began to get restless. The prisoners in the tent were full of wine, which they had sneaked in. Every now and then one tried to get out and I'd have to order him back at the point of the bayonet. This, toward comrades with whom one has fought as we had fought at Mousseifré, is a hard job.

Ten o'clock came, and still I was not relieved. The Turkish sergeant came and I asked to be relieved. He ordered me to stay on. We had quite an argument. He threatened to tell the lieutenant. "Go and tell the lieutenant," I said. "Guard duty is two hours, and I have been on four."

"Well, stay there."

"All right," I said, "I'll stay, but I won't be responsible. Guard duty is two hours; I have been on four. I'll stay here, but I won't be responsible."

The sergeant left, and I walked over to Sylvestre Budney who had been cooking for the section since Mousseifré, where our cook had been killed. He was pulverizing coffee grains on a flat stone with the heel of his rifle, the Legion's coffee-mill. I lit a cigarette, and just then our old friend Gorigas, the drunken terror, crawled out of the prison tent and stood before me.

"I want to go to the town," he said belligerently.

"I don't care where you go," I said. "You had better stay here, but if you want to go, I won't stop you."

He stood there quite a while; he could not believe his ears. Then he gave a grin, and well pleased, started off down the road.

I still stayed on guard, unrelieved, and still did nothing to keep the prisoners from going. At four, when the sergeant of the day came, two thirds of the prisoners were gone. He started to roar at me, and I gave my same answer. I had been on guard since six in the morning, since ten I had not considered myself responsible. He threatened to report me to the lieutenant. "*Tell* the lieutenant; *je m'en fiche*," I said.

By five o'clock, most of the prisoners had staggered back. But no Gorigas. By eight reports came in that he was in a canteen, raving drunk, fighting off every one, his knife out, threatening to carve up everybody. As usual, Sergeant d'Etienne was sent for. "I'll get him," said d'Etienne.

He went down to the canteen, entered, went up to Gorigas—who stood holding a girl with one arm, brandishing his knife with the other.

"*Tiens*, Gorigas! Have a drink."

"*Bien sûr*, *mon sergent*, I'll have a drink with you."

They drank. "*A mon tour*," said Gorigas, and they had another drink.

"Now, come with me, Gorigas," said d'Etienne quietly.

"*Bien sûr*, *mon sergent*, I'll go with you. I'd go anywhere with you, *mon sergent*."

And following d'Etienne, he walked back into prison.

If ever the sergeants reported me to Lieutenant Vernon, I heard nothing of it. That guard duty should be for two hours only at one time is a tradition in the Legion for which the men fight jealously.

Our "long" rest in Ghazalé lasted just three days. On the third day we "touched" rations. The column was starting out again in the morning on a punitive expedition. From the very amount of the rations we drew, we knew we were going into a wild country, and we swore when we saw what we would have to pack in our *musettes*, and on our backs. Each man drew four of the enormous *boules* of bread, of which one half *boule* is a day's ration. On top of that six days' biscuit ration, two cans of *singe*, two kilos of chocolate, coffee, and soup tablets. In the morning we were off for Mousseifré. And here—where there were no canteens and when there would not be any for a while—in subtle appreciation of our conduct in Ghazalé, we received our pay! Mine by this time as a *bleu* in Syria, amounted to the munificent sum of twenty-two francs fifty centimes every two weeks.

The column of which we were a part was a good deal the same as that which had relieved Suweida, consisting of all arms—tirailleurs, spahis, Syrian *Partisans*, artillery, cavalry, both regular and irregular. As a novelty we dragged along a column of some two thousand camels, traveling tied tail-to-head by sixes or twelves, each animal bearing two barrels of water slung on its high pack saddle. The duty of the punitive column was to comb the land, and punish the *villages insoumis*—the villages that were in revolt.

This we did by pillaging and burning, moving in a great circle from the right of Mousseifré to the left. What generally happened was this.

As we approached the village, the Druses would attack us at long range. There would be an exchange of rifle fire as we moved up; bullets would whizz over our heads or stir dust at our feet, then suddenly all this would cease.

Coming to the village, we camped around it in a great circle, and the mounted spahis would ride in to reconnoitre. If they reported the village empty, which was usually the case, the tirailleurs then went in and did the work. They drove away the cattle and the sheep, then set the village on fire. When it was fiercely burning we marched on.

The Legionaires were not used at this work. We were always in advance guard, or flank guard, or perched somewhere guarding some one or something from surprise. Some of us on the whole were glad for this, but often did Delaporte, and Gorigas, and Kurtzman and others swear softly as they thought of the good time they might have had if we had gone into the village with the tirailleurs. They felt they could show them something—and I am sure that they would have, especially Delaporte, a past grand master at all the arts of campaigning, and what the French call a great "débrouillard."

Every morning, from the big aviation camps behind us, planes came across the sky and joined the column, scouting up there in great circlings and sudden darts and swoops that looked like play. The Druses shot at them with their rifles, and actually brought one down now and then. You would see the plane descend and land suddenly, and burst into flames. Sometimes the aviator was able to fall among us and be saved; sometimes he fell in the *bled* and was slaughtered before we could get to him.

Thus in a great circle from west to east we went, burning and pillaging the *villages insoumis*, and impressing the others with the show of our strength.

The column was a light column; we marched hard and fast, and our rations grew more and more meager. One day, our battalion was in advance guard moving along the plain parallel to the mountains, half way up which a village was perched. Suddenly we were ordered to turn at right angles and take the village. We turned and were met by Druse fire. For a while we answered, from behind rocks and stones, then the fire being ineffective, got impatient and charged up the hill. Up the hill went the Vingt-neuvième, over hedges, through trees, yelling like Apaches, Lieutenant Vernon at our head, brandishing his automatic, the *adjudant-chef* at his side. Finally we came to a little house, then a stone wall, and stopped right there. It was a magnificent wall, thick, almost chin high, and we saw where we might save ourselves our usual cruel labor *aux murailles*. And we did. The house, the orchard and its walls, which were to one side of the village, promptly became a *poste* in the encircling, and here we camped.

Our rations had been low for some time, we were hungry and we were gaunt, when a bit of good luck fell to us. A squad of mounted spahis were driving some sheep out of the village. Delaporte leaped the wall, ran over, seized one of the sheep, threw it over his shoulder and ran back with it to us. The spahis came after, protesting. They wanted their mutton. But Delaporte was firm. "The sheep belong to us as well as to them," he argued with good logic. "Don't we do our share of fighting? And where do the sheep come, except out of the fighting?" As a matter of form the "*sous-offs*" told him to give back the sheep, but he couldn't see it at all that way, and the spahis withdrew, leaving ba-ba in our hands.

Things were looking up. I went hunting in the garden, and found tomatoes, pumpkins, cucumbers and melons, which we took up to the kitchens. Herschkorn flushed a chicken and ran it down. Some one investigated the farm-house, and came out yelling. A room in there was packed full of onions!

We had a feast that night. Pepi, the Marseillais, cooked it for us, braising the mutton with onions in a huge casserole. There were tomatoes and cucumbers for salad (we didn't bother to make a salad) and melon for dessert. We ate till we could hardly get up again.

The next day, we were down to the "ordinary" again, which in this campaign was about nothing. We killed a mule, and the pieces were distributed, each man cooking his own, frying it with onions. The column was camped in a great crescent of five kilometers below us. We were waiting for a convoy of ammunition and provisions from Mousseifré. We could see it in the distance, trying to get through to us. Clouds of smoke could be seen rising. It never did get through, and later we learned with sorrow that the Druses had captured the camion carrying our pay and another laden with cigarettes.

That night the Druses attacked in force. I was standing guard at the wall at about ten o'clock and the night was bitterly cold. I knew there were Druses prowling around; every now and then I would hear a stone dislodged. Suddenly a bullet sang by over my head, and simultaneously the night was full of the little fiery stabs of discharged rifles. I yelled "Aux armes," the sergeant, who had been sleeping at my feet, rose; everybody rose and a pretty scrap began. The Senegalese to our right were also being attacked, and were yelling like devils. Then the entire column, camped in a huge crescent, opened up—a beautiful sight what with the thousands and thousands of rifle flashes. The artillery came into action, the shells bursting beautifully on the mountainside. For a time, this was war as it should be!

The next morning we were standing around

our wall, eating "monkey" fried with onions and talking the usual Legion conversation, "I wish I were in Damascus, I'd be doing this or that," or "I wish I were in Beirut, there's a certain young person there," etc., or "Ever been in Saïgon? That's the place. You do this and that" —the legionaire is always wishing himself elsewhere than where he is. Along came a young lieutenant from the Tirailleurs, a young shavetail fresh from St. Cyr or the Polytechnique, all spick and span and elegant. We saluted, he saluted and stopped curious over our *déjeuner*. "*Bonjour, les légionnaires, comment ça va-t-il?*" "*Très bien, mon lieutenant. Et vous, mon lieutenant, comment allez-vous?*" "*Très bien, les légionnaires*—and what is it you are eating here?" "Just a little *singe*, *mon lieutenant*, but we have onions!" He hesitated upon going, you could see his nostrils twitch. "Won't you have a little, *mon lieutenant?*" said Delaporte. "*Non, non,*" said the lieutenant hastily. "Your rations are meager enough as it is." But he could not quite tear himself away. "*Mais si, mon lieutenant,*" cried Delaporte, "you must have some. It's good, you just see." He ran over to the kitchen, got a clean *gamelle*, put in it some of the *singe* cooked in onion, on it a hunk of bread, got a knife and a fork and brought it to the lieutenant. He tried to eat slowly, but you could see he was terribly hungry. "What is the matter with the *popotte* [the officers' mess]?" said Delaporte, always at his ease. "Don't you have good things to eat?" "Our *popotte?*" said the lieutenant. "Not on this campaign. All we've had is *singe*. And without onions."

"*Nom de Dieu!*" swore Delaporte after the lieutenant had gone, "what a column! Even the officers starving!"

As for him, he never starved. He was the exemplary "débrouillard." He had always something in his *musette*, and in garrison, money for wine.

The column was here two days, and then marched on its way to Mezra, where on August 12, General Michaud's column of four thousand men had been surprised by the Druses and practically annihilated. But this place where we had camped had become known by this time as Zwiebelberg, or Onion Hill. As Zwiebelberg it is still known and thus written down on the maps.

CHAPTER XI

WHEN at early dawn the column marched away from Onion Hill, we Legionaires,—the Eighteenth and Nineteenth Companies of the First Régiment de Marche, together with my company, the Vingt-neuvième de Marche, were its rear flank guard. Well away to the right and the rear of the convoy, we marched in file, five paces between men, so that a simple order of half turn would find us all deployed in skirmish line, facing the enemy. Out beyond was a screen of mounted Moroccan spahis.

We had hardly left our walls and stones before we came into a harassing fire. We could see the Druses on the crests above us, in their black jackets and baggy trousers, their square black cloths flapping on their necks, and now and then a horseman dashing out into the open and under cover. Bullets sang over us and kicked up dust at our feet.

As the column moved on, the attack continued, and our battalion became one of *décrochage*, of "unhooking." It was our job to continuously "unhook" the column from the harassing enemy.

After we had marched thus a little way, my squad, with an automatic rifle, was ordered to a little pile of stones. There were eight of us—Tokar, who was the *adjudant-chef;* Corporal Costanovitch, the big Russian; the German Kupe; Bolse, an Alsatian, who handled the automatic rifle; Brix, the Austrian; Budney, the Pole; and Herschkorn, the little Parisian. We settled ourselves behind the little pile of stones, with the automatic drove off the Druses, then, picking it up and ourselves, ran and caught up with the company.

This kept up for about an hour and a half. Our squad would hold a pile of stones while the rest of the company went on; we would drive back the Druses, then run and catch up again—hard work, you may believe. Meanwhile the cavalry was keeping the Druses engaged off on the right flank.

Thus we arrived before Rezzas, and the spahis, ahead, having been sniped at from the village, set it on fire. As the flames and smoke began to rise, and the roofs to crackle, suddenly the battle became a serious one.

The Druses drove in the cavalry screen, which passed among us on the run, dismounted and henceforth fought as infantry. As our battalion stopped to hold the attack, the Senegalese, who were flank guard ahead of us—we being rear flank guard—kept on going, leaving a gap through which we were in danger of being enveloped. At the same time the Druses jumped the rear guard of tirailleurs, and came in among us.

My squad at the time was at the job it had had all morning, occupying a position with the automatic. And that position at the time was a precarious one.

We lay near the top of a crest, with a slope going down before us, and this slope was all of earth beaten down hard, with no stone and no cover of any kind. We had simply put down our sacks before our noses. Right behind us, in a defile beneath the crest, the convoy was passing, or trying to pass—camions, trucks, *automobiles blindés*, camel trains, mules, all the impedimenta of the column. The defile turned sharply at this point, the convoy had become entangled, bullets were falling into it, and disorder reigned, with horses kicking and screaming, big trucks falling into ruts, men swearing and sweating.

We lay on top of the crest, on the hard-beaten ground, with no shelter, with this behind us. Ahead of us the ground dropped to a dry waterway, then rose again, this time all covered with rocks and stones and hedges, to a crest also rocky and giving protection. Up there on the crest were the Druses, pouring their fire down upon us, and charging now and then from stone to stone down the slope, leaping from cover to cover. From moment to moment they were getting bolder. Along the crest a horseman would come bursting, dismount, fire a few rounds, jump on his horse and run along as if in a movie at forty miles an hour. But what gave us more trouble were the wild infantrymen, leaping down the slope from cover to cover, to come almost within hand-to-hand distance, and hurl at us their potato-mashers.

Our squad was lying in a line thus: Lieutenant Vernon was at the left end, coolly directing the fire with his binoculars. Next lay Tokar, the *adjudant-chef*, then came Costanovitch and Kupe. In the center, Bolse was firing the Chauchat automatic. To his right lay Brix, whom we always called Brixey, then myself, then my *copain* Budney, then Herschcorn. Budney to my right was swearing as he shot, as was his way, but Brixey was firing slowly and carefully. He was a fine shot and took his time and tried always to get his man.

After a time I heard the *adjudant-chef* roaring from his end of the line. "Brixey, Brixey, *nom de Dieu;* fire more quickly. This isn't firing school. Fire fast!"

But Brixey evidently was firing no faster, for again the *adjudant-chef* roared down the line. "Brixey! *Nom de Dieu*, fire, I tell you! *Nom de Dieu*, is he asleep? Wake him up, Clare!"

Now it was the habit of Brixey, old Legionaire that he was, to go to sleep whenever possible; and several times he had been known to take a snooze on the firing line.

So I crawled over a few feet to Brixey. He seemed to be asleep all right. I reached over and tapped him on the shoulder. He did not awaken. I clutched his shoulder and shook him. Then I saw that my hand was covered with blood. He was slumping strangely with his head upon his sack. He was not asleep, he was dead. A bullet had severed his carotid artery; he had died there without a whisper.

"Brixey can't fire, *mon adjudant*," I shouted back. "*Il est mort.*"

Just then the automatic jammed and went out of action. Brixey's sack was a *sac spécial* holding the automatic's ammunition, and to make up in part for the extra weight, instead of the regular Lebel, he had been carrying a light carbine which was an extremely fine shooting gun. The adjutant shouted to me: "Clare, take Brixey's carbine and all his ammunition and bring them to Corporal Costanovitch." I crawled along the line with the cartridges and carbine. The carbine was given to Bolse, who had been shooting the now useless automatic, and the two hundred and fifty cartridges were divided among us. We needed them, we were running out of ammunition.

I crawled back to my place and we continued shooting, stretched out there in the open behind our sacks, the convoy in uproar behind us, trying hard to extricate itself, the Druses before us, firing and yelling, rushing down the slope and throwing their grenades. To our right the Eighteenth Company of our battalion was being badly cut up, and twice already had come to grips using the bayonet.

After a while the *adjudant-chef* called me. "Clare, *viens ici.*" I crawled along behind the others till up to him. "Get behind the lieutenant," he said, "and listen well to what he says." So I crawled on till I was right behind Lieutenant Vernon.

"Go down the hill to the adjutant of the Eighteenth," he said, "and try to find Lieutenant Laffite."

Lieutenant Laffite was in charge of the battalion's company of machine-guns:

"Find Lieutenant Laffite," said Lieutenant Vernon, "and ask him if we can't have a machine-gun quickly. That I don't think we can hold them off much longer without a machine-gun. Do you understand?"

"Yes, my lieutenant."

"Repeat the order."

I repeated it. "*Bien*," he said. "Go as soon as you can make it."

I started off without my rifle. "No, take your gun," he said.

I picked up the gun and started walking. "No,"

he said, "you will never make it that way. You must crawl."

But I couldn't see myself crawling all that distance, and told him so.

"*Bien*," he said, and, "tutoying" me, "*Comme tu veux*, *alors*—as you wish it, then."

And I set out walking down the hill.

It was exactly like a rain storm, or a hail storm. Bullets kicked up the dirt all around me. But I kept on just as I was, just walking. And the reason I was not running wasn't courage: it was weariness. I was so tired I could not run. Fear of death could not make me run. Nothing at all could have made me run. I was too tired.

I got down, found the adjutant, and finally Lieutenant Laffite, and gave him the message. He was a little fellow, cool as a cucumber. "*Bien, bien*," he said, a bit like a school teacher bothered by many children. "I'll go up with you and view the position, and see what we can do. Machine-guns are not growing on the bushes."

So I went back the way I had come, and he with me, to where Lieutenant Vernon lay directing the fire. They discussed the situation for a moment, and then a bullet got Laffite right in the ankle. "*Sacré nom de Dieu*," he swore, "I'm going to the ambulance." And without more ado started hopping down toward the convoy. He was a comical sight. He'd hop along ten or twelve feet, try the bad leg, find he couldn't stand the pain, and hop on again on one leg, a little bit of a fellow, going as fast as a gnome.

And we didn't get our machine-gun. The men of the machine-gun section had all been killed or wounded as usual.

Many men were getting killed. A corporal near by got shot through the heart. Didier, a big drummer from Paris, got it right between the eyes. The Eighteenth was using the bayonet now and then. But we were beating off the Druses all the same.

Meanwhile it was getting lonely up there. The convoy had been extricated and was gone; there was nothing behind us. The Senegalese had gone on, we had only a gap to our left. Everybody had gone on leaving us here. Up came a staff officer, furious and out of breath. "What in hell are you doing here?" he roared to Vernon.

"We've had no orders to move," Vernon answered quietly. "We were told to hold here; we've had no orders since; we're still here."

"Well, you have your orders now. Scoot!"

So it was "Debout! A l'arrière! Pas gymnastique!" We sprang to our feet, seized our sacks and started after the column on the double-quick. Just as Herschcorn picked his sack, a bullet went through his knee, another through his ankle. He staggered, went down, got up, then went down again. I reached for him, but Sergeant d'Etienne was already there. Taking his sack, putting his arm about him, he was half dragging, half carrying him along.

We went on after the column, the Vingt-neuvième and Nineteenth ahead, the Eighteenth covering. The Druses seemed half glad we were going; we were glad we were going; it was a case of mutual satisfaction. But we were leaving poor old Brixey up there; we were leaving all our dead. And among them, one that was not yet dead.

This was a German of the Eighteenth who, when in garrison, was always *chef des douches*, chief of the showers. His was the job of heating the water, of keeping the showers clean. And we used to josh him because he always had his letters addressed from his home far away, to "Hans Rhine, Chef des Douches." His German parents did not know what this meant, and no doubt thought it was some sort of high rank which their son had gained. In the midst of the action he got a bullet in the stomach. He had always been a cheerful companion, he sang on the march, every one liked him, and several of his comrades now tried to get him to the camion that was serving as ambulance. But he refused to be moved.

The captain of the Eighteenth came along and argued with him. "Come, come, Hans, let us get you to the ambulance."

But he lay there, obdurate. "*Non, non, mon capitaine*, let me be. I cannot stand to be moved. I would suffer too much. No, no, it is *fini*. Just let me lie here. *Fini* the fighting, *fini* hunger and thirst and the *corvées*, *fini* the long marches in the sun. *C'est fini*. I cannot stand to be moved. Please, *mon capitaine*, let me lie here, and let me have my rifle."

It is against the rule under any circumstance to leave a rifle or any weapon behind which can be of use to the enemy. But the captain of the Eighteenth let Hans keep his rifle. And now for a time as we retreated on the double-quick, we could hear him firing down there against the Druses closing in. There was a last shot, and then silence. There is no doubt that Hans used this last shot on himself.

When we had gone a little way, our company dropped back to cover, and the Eighteenth, which had been covering, passed by us. And the very last man of it was their captain, firing with a carbine as any common soldier. I'll always remember him—a little black bearded man. His left arm had almost been shot off, and aiming he laid the carbine right across the wound. His face, which had been bronzed with the sun, now drained of blood, was a saffron yellow, so that his black beard showed blacker than ink. Along he went, at the very rear of his company, covering it with his carbine, firing across his bleeding arm.

We caught up to the column in the plain. The Druses had not followed: they rarely fought us on the flat. The column at sundown reached the village of Aéré. And the general, on an order declaring that the Legion that day had saved the column, ordered that we camp in the very center of it, protected on all sides with no walls to build and no guard to mount. Which we did—having a good night's sleep—which we had earned. For this affair the battalion and my company were cited in the general orders of the army, its second citation in a few weeks, and one which won it the right to wear the fourragère. And I—as I was to find out later—was cited and granted the croix de guerre. Just for that little promenade in search of a machine-gun.

That evening after *la soupe*, Sylvestre Budney, the young Pole who was a *bleu* in my squad, came to me. Brixey, who had been killed this day, had been his *copain*, his buddy. "Will you be my *copain* now?" he asked like a school boy, and I said I would be his *copain*. This is a serious relation in the Legion; with your *copain* you share your cigarettes, the contents of your *bidon*, of your *musette*, everything you have; you stay side by side in the fight; you give up your life if it is needed to help him; he is your brother.

THE AUTHOR AFTER A DAY OF SKIRMISHING

A TYPICAL OUTPOST OF THE LEGION

A STRONGHOLD OF THE DRUSES

A GROUP OF TIRAILLEURS WHO FOUGHT WITH US AGAINST THE DRUSES

FRENCH SPAHIS, THE COSSACKS OF THE DESERT

REBEL DRUSES

ENTRANCE TO THE "POSTE DE POLICE"

A TYPICAL LEGIONAIRE ATTACHED TO THE CAMEL CORPS

CHAPTER XII

THE day after the affair at Rezzas, we went on to Mezra where, in August, General Michaud's column of four thousand men, marching to the relief of Suweida, had been overwhelmed by the Druses and destroyed. This was the first time the army had been able to get near the place since that day.

We camped near where the ill-fated column had camped—a sad sort of place, in a bowl of the hills. The ground was still black and ravaged as though it had burned. Twisted remains of burned *automobiles blindés* and ambulances and camions were everywhere and skeletons in them. There were traces still of the low ineffective stone walls which the doomed column had put up, and within them and about them, strewing the ground on all sides, bones of the dead men mixed with twisted remnants of automatics and machine-guns.

Details were put out to clean up, to gather bones and bury them. But my company, held in screen, did not participate in this terrible toil.

Serving with the Senegalese camping near us was a Franco-Englishman from the island of Guernsey who had been with the Michaud column that day, and who told me what had happened. It seemed that Michaud, who had a good record from the World War, but who was unaccustomed to this kind of warfare, had marched all the way in column of threes, with a small advance guard two kilometers ahead, and a rear guard two kilometers behind. All the way they had been harassed by the Druses, and when they reached Mezra, there were already many wounded in the ambulance trucks.

Going into camp, they had put up insufficient walls, low enough to be leaped by horses. And they had hardly put these up before the Druses had come storming in from all sides, foot and horse. The camps had been *enfoncés*, liaison was lost, disorder reigned. The artillery had been jumped, and its commandant had shot himself. Soon the *automobiles blindés* got out of ammunition; the Druses, climbing upon them, would thrust their long knives and sabers through the slits and butcher the drivers and helpless occupants, then, taking the gasoline, set them on fire. They had set on fire the ambulance trucks filled with wounded. And finally, seeing that all was lost, the commander had given the word "Sauve qui peut."

The survivors had then broken and fled. Or rather, singly or in small groups had tried to fight their way back to Bosra. All alone, fighting all the way, the man who was now telling us this had made Bosra, arriving there more dead than alive.

That night, at dusk, I was sitting by my section's fire making some *ravio* coffee (*ravio* is anything extra, obtained by means ingenious and illegitimate) for Budney and me while he was out drawing our rations. We of course never had fires at night, but I thought the fire was too low to show and that the night had not quite set in. Suddenly there was a discharge up the hill, and several hatfuls of bullets landed together in the glowing ashes. It did not take us long to put that fire out.

At night, as I was standing guard, the Druses jumped our camp. We drove them off, and a moment later they attacked the next camp. All night they went around, attacking one camp after the other, circling the column. Machine-guns were going off all the time, several times the seventy-fives spoke, Véry flares were in the air: we had a poor night's sleep.

But that was the end of the expedition. The next day we marched back to Mousseifré. We arrived at night, in rags, out of ammunition, dog-tired. And our sergeant, d'Etienne, went out scouting, somewhere bought a bottle of cherry brandy for which he paid twenty francs, passed it around, a *quart* to each man, upon which we gladly wrapped ourselves in our blankets and went supperless to bed. The place, by the way, had at last been cleaned out, the Druse bodies burned so that we could now sleep.

By the next day we were back to Ghazalé for a rest; we reëquipped, bathed, washed our clothes. While resting there we acted as guard to a convoy for Bosra—a quiet duty but with plenty of the usual marching, thirst and hunger of course, but brightened by one little festivity.

On this march we had reached Mousseifré, at dark, and with very little to eat. Budney and I were hungry, so we strolled over to the trucks and bummed from the drivers a little soup and bread. When it was dark the *adjudant-chef* called for volunteers to go get the battalion's rations from the food dump. Budney nudged me. "Volunteer, volunteer," he whispered, "you may be able to swipe something to eat."

So I volunteered, together with several Poles, and at one-thirty in the morning we went with our pack mules to the stores. We went over to the stores and drew the regular rations for the battalion. But in the darkness we were drawing other things. A Pole passed me a great loaf of bread, in another moment, another. Suddenly came a flock of sardines. Then the cans of *singe*. All this was not going into the saddle-packs, but into the *musettes*. When we returned we had a dozen of the great bread loaves, a whole case of sardines, twelve cans of *singe*. We awoke Budney to tell him, and had quite a nice *déjeuner*.

Upon our return from this convoying, the battalion was ordered to Damascus. At least, Damascus we thought it was, and our anticipations of a gay easy life ran high. As a matter of fact we were quartered in the *caserne* of the Syrian gendarmes at Kadem, a suburb, and found we were not allowed to go into Damascus proper. Kadem, however, was a pleasant place. The land was peopled and rich; we were amidst olive groves, and truck gardens growing tomatoes, lettuce, onions and melons. The water was plentiful and good, and we rested.

We took part in a pleasant little punitive expedition on our second day here. There was a small village about five kilometers away, on the railroad, and some of its inhabitants lately had taken to the amusement of sniping at the military trains as they passed. Two or three men had been killed and several more wounded. The *caïd* had been ordered to produce the guilty. He had answered in the usual dilatory oriental manner. There had not been any shooting. If there had, he did not know who had done it. And anyway he did not know where they were hiding; he could not produce them.

So on this fine morning, we set out—our battalion, a battalion of tirailleurs, a battery of seventy-fives, and a squadron of mounted Moroccan spahis. We came to the village. It was a wealthy little village, very different from the eagle nests we were used to up in the mountains; we could see orchards and gardens, corrals with sheep and goats. We encircled it, and the spahis rode in, together with an interpreter and an officer to demand an indemnity.

We waited outside, laying bets, hoping, the pessimists predicting the indemnity would be paid. After a while the spahis rode out with the officer and the interpreter. The indemnity had been asked and refused. Another half hour's grace had been given in case the *caïd* would change his mind.

Evidently he was not changing it, for the population, singly or in groups, was beating it out of the village. When most of them had gone, a few fanatics who had remained opened fire on us. The tirailleurs got out their machine-guns and shut them up.

The half hour had gone now. And it was my own company which was ordered into the village to do the work! I can still see the look of "I can't believe it; it's too good to be true" that came over some of my comrades' faces. "En avant, marche," and we marched in.

There never existed anywhere, I think, any body of men more efficient for the work there was to do here than the Vingt-neuvième de Marche. The tradition is that in such a foray, all that is food goes to every one, is shared among the kitchens of the different outfits. But if anything else is found, that is the finder's business: he keeps it. Squads of men went about beating down doors with the butts of their rifles, flowing into the houses. You could tell of their progress through the house by the crash of glass and crockery, the crash of furniture being destroyed. It was a wealthy village; there seemed to be many plate-glass mirrors; the Legionaires would attack them with the same joy one sometimes sees in firemen under similar circumstances. Then with everything reduced to kindling inside, they'd pour out, laden with linens and sometimes silks, with bracelets and spangles and knick-knacks, with great jars of honey and blocks of dried raisins, with watches and with clocks, with God knows what. Outside, the streets ran with herded sheep and goats, with donkeys and mules and bullocks. One man had found a blooded mare, another a fine stallion.

As for me, together with the *adjudant-chef* of the company, I was after chicken, ducks and geese. I had finally twenty-nine chickens and one goose all in one huge chaplet, and a donkey to carry them. But when it came time to get out, the donkey would not carry them. That is to say, he was willing to carry them, but not willing to move with them. I couldn't get him to budge. I twisted his tail, I tried everything; stubbornly loyal to the village of his childhood, or perhaps simply stiff with principles that forbade him to aid in any such mission as this, he squared his little hoofs, put his ears and his weight back, and remained where he was. So finally with a parting kick I left him there, myself carrying my goose and twenty-nine hens. Have you ever carried a goose and twenty-nine hens? It is much more of a task than it appears in the reading of it. One is always toiling in the Legion.

Meanwhile Budney, taken along by the *adjudant-chef* of the battalion, was busy at another matter. The two men, going into each house successively after the looters were through, were pouring kerosene over the floors and the walls, and touching a match to it. When, looking like some migrating pastoral people of bygone days on the move, we marched off carrying with us our loot, driving before us our cattle, behind us the village was starting to burn fiercely under great clouds of smoke.

Back at Kadem we feasted for three days.

Feasting, however, is not long the Legion life. A few days after we were again on the march, toward the mountains again. After two days' heavy marching we reached Kinetra, a village allotted to the Tcherkess, irregular cavalry of Mohammedan Russians who were fighting with the French. Here a column was formed of a few battalions of Senegalese, three battalions of tirailleurs, two batteries of light mountain artillery, and our battalion. And we marched on into the mountains of the Liban for three days and laid siege to Hasbya.

Hasbya was at the top of a rocky hill, and was strongly entrenched, barbed-wired and supplied with machine-guns and ammunition. The three days we spent before it were some of the most miserable I passed in the Legion. It was in November; we were in a bitterly cold fog all the time; we had had to dig trenches, and the fire from the town was such we could hardly ever raise a nose out of them. The commander of the expedition was not so good. We felt we could have charged right into the town and finished the business; instead we were held to the miserable trenches. But finally a flock of planes came over, severely bombed the town—and to our surprise, and our satisfaction, it then surrendered.

In explanation of some of the scenes which

have been described, it must be explained that the Legionaire is almost always hungry. Even in garrison, his rations are just enough to keep him alive and active. They are calculated to keep him gaunt and fine; the Legion doesn't care for a fat soldier. This condition is aggravated of course when campaigning.

Our rations consisted of a half loaf of bread a day; a little beef or mutton when it could be obtained, or of *singe* when it couldn't; soup, and either lentils, beans or macaroni; three cups of coffee a day, and one *quart* of wine. The *quart* is not a quart, it is a quarter of a liter, a quarter of one quart. When meat was not obtainable, *singe*, canned beef, took its place. When neither lentils, macaroni, nor beans were in the larder, a piece of chocolate would be substituted. In his *musette* the marching Legionaire was supposed to always carry emergency rations consisting of a can of *singe*, a few soup tablets, and a third of a bar of chocolate.

In winter we carried one blanket, just long enough to cover a man of my size from neck to ankles. In summer we carried none at all and slept in our capotes. The capote, the overcoat, we carried always. The easiest way to carry it—

what with the tremendously heavy pack which is the Legionaire's—was by wearing it. But we suffered inside of it on marches in summer, in the desert, under a torrid sun.

It was marching back from Hasbya that I destroyed a bridge. We had camped that night at the top of a hill, and when we finished our walls, we could find no wood for cooking. It was nearly always my job to get wood, and the *adjudant-chef* as usual put me on this *corvée* that night. I combed the hill carefully; I could find no wood. But at the bottom of the hill, where our road wound, was a stream, and here I found a bridge. It was made of five great logs, spiked together with smaller pieces, and just wide enough to allow the passing of a camion. I went back to camp and asked for more men. Our captain (we had a captain now, a Breton called Ourieux) was in bad humor, waiting for his supper which did not seem to be coming, and the detail was readily lent me. We went back to the bridge, and by dint of ingenuity and hard work, managed to pry off one of the big end logs, and rolled it up the hill to the camp of the First Section, where the others could get at it with their axes. "*C'est bien ça,*" the adjutant said, "where did you find that?" "It's from the bridge down there," I said modestly, and he laughed. The captain, now sure of his supper, came around. "Where did you get it?" he asked. "From the bridge down there," I said. He looked at me, rubbed his hands and laughed. When morning came, and the camions started down the road, they soon came to the bridge, and it was now too narrow to be crossed. Splashing and roaring across the water they'd have to go. And the colonel of the column came to pay us a visit. "*Sacrée légion!*" he roared. "Band of bandits!" Our captain stood there, rubbing his hands, pulling at his whiskers, chuckling, and not answering a word under the storm.

CHAPTER XIII

BACK we went to Damascus. And if any of us held still expectations of a luxurious oriental life, we lost them as we came into the city.

We marched in with loaded rifles, with grenades in our *musettes*, and with orders to shoot any civilian who molested us. Between Kadem and the city proper we passed the maidan, or Druse quarter. The French, losing patience, had bombarded it. The roof of the long bazar street was like a sieve with machine-gun bullet holes; houses here and there lay pulverized by the seventy-fives.

Barricades lined the streets in Damascus proper; barbed-wire entanglements; at nearly every corner was a blockhouse with a machine-gun post.

Our quarters were in the stables, at the foot of the citadel, right in the center of town. The citadel seventy-fives were sending shells over the city, and into villages beyond.

Every night there would be shooting all about

us. At night the Druses, or bandits from the hills, filtered in; joined by some of the native inhabitants, they would snipe at the French foreigners. A gendarme told me of having seen a European killed right at the door of the American consulate; and the invisible sniper had been so near that the gendarme had heard distinctly the snapping of his rifle lock.

When morning came, the treacherous inhabitants would slip back to their homes, and the bandits from the hills would filter out into what is called the gardens of Damascus—the olive groves and orchards, the farms, all surrounded with high stone walls, which lie about the city. Patrols were shot at from roofs, from cellars. Sentinels would have their throats cut at their posts. Fighting went on from house to house, from street to street. It was a savage, internal warfare, with no quarter from either side.

In a few days our battalion joined a column sent around the city to clear the "gardens."

For three days we marched and marched on the outskirts of the city, potted at all of the time, and finding nothing. A few natives surprised carrying arms were summarily shot; a village was pillaged and burned. But we went through the olive gardens, the farms, the forest without being able to establish contact, yet being shot at all of the time. The mounted spahis with us were almost wild at their inability to find the snipers. We finally returned, having accomplished nothing.

We were then garrisoned at Kadem, a suburb. One morning my *copain* Budney and I were across the street from the *caserne*, washing our shirts in a stream that flowed by there, when shooting broke out over in Damascus. At first we paid no attention. But the sound of the shooting was spreading toward us—and suddenly a hail of bullets sprinkled the ground about us.

We picked up our wash, and with the few clothes we had on, beat it for the *caserne*.

Every one in there had seized his rifle by this time, and we were firing back at will. Our captain, our two lieutenants had gone to town; we were without officers. But without officers, we took it into our heads to charge. Yelling like Indians we sallied, drove out the snipers from the gardens about, then darted back to the *caserne*, which was a big stone building easy to defend.

But as time went on and still the shooting continued, and we heard nothing from our officers, the thing became serious. Our *adjudant-chef* was getting white-haired.

And suddenly in came our captain, purple-faced, storming and furious. He had come in on the street car, and the street car had been shot at all the way. The motorman had tried to stop several times, and to hide under the car, but one of our company, a big German *vaguemestre* sergeant, had placed a pistol at his ear and ordered him on. Along the street the car had whizzed, shot at from the houses on both sides, the few Legionaires in it firing back out of the windows. And the captain was furious. Some muleteers who had been in town came back at the same time. They had had to fight their way back; and three of them had been killed and several wounded. This increased the captain's fury. He went to the telephone, which strangely enough, in all this pother, was still working, and called up the citadel. "Send down a half dozen tanks," he asked.

In an hour five little whippet tanks came rumbling down the road, wheeled, and lined up in front of the *caserne;* an immaculate artillery lieutenant came in. He was a young lad, who laughed at everything. By this time the shooting had all stopped and everything seemed quiet as could be. "What is it, *mon capitaine?*" said the lieutenant soothingly. "What is it we can do for you with our tanks?"

"They have shot at me, they have shot at my men. They have killed some of my muleteers," roared the captain still angry. "See if you can knock down a few of those houses over there, and give us a clear space."

"Très bien," the lieutenant laughed. He went back to his tanks, and they began spitting. Using their little thirty-seven millimeter guns, they sent shell after shell into the houses from which there had been firing on us. These were mostly of clay strengthened with wood. They would crumble and collapse at each precisely placed shell, while we, all at the windows as if at the theater, amused ourselves, and our captain, walking to and fro, rubbed his hands in satisfaction. "C'est bien, ça," he would say, as a house sat down in a cloud of its own dust. "C'est bien, ça."

When he had been satisfied, and a large enough space had been cleared about the *caserne* to make us safe from such future attacks, the lieutenant saluted, shook hands, and the little tanks went rumbling back to Damascus.

It was a fine rest we were getting in Damascus. The next day the battalion set out again. The Eighteenth and the Nineteenth Companies were to be established in posts which, with ours, would encircle Damascus. We marched all night and most of the next day, shot at continuously from behind trees, from behind walls, from houses, by an invisible enemy we could not get at, whom our spahis seldom caught. Any one captured with arms was placed against a wall and shot by a firing squad. Such firing squads were made up of volunteers. I never volunteered, but several of the hard eggs of my company did. A village on the way was pillaged and burned. The wild Tcherkess irregulars who screened for us got out of hand; you could hear the screams of women; it was pretty bad. When we had got to the site of the new post of the Eighteenth, we labored like convicts at its walls. And leaving it we had to fight back all the way. The Nineteenth Company in turn was left at a post, which we had to build. Then the Vingt-neuvième marched back into Kadem, worn out. We were by this time down to about sixty men.

A week later we went out to provision the Eighteenth and Nineteenth in their posts. We fought all the way as we went through the pretty country, with its walnut trees and poplars, almost like France. That is to say, all the way we were shot at without being able to get at anything in particular. The Eighteenth had been isolated since we had left them, and when we came we fell on each others' necks. We had to fight still harder to get at the Nineteenth, but we did. Again great hails, slaps on shoulders, "embrassades" between old friends. Then off we marched.

As we slogged along on our return, with a bullet singing every now and then, or caterwauling at our feet, we came suddenly under much more heavy fire. The source of it was located after a while. A village up on the side of a hill, and hidden from us by a small forest, was blazing away at us.

The colonel of our column was fed up. He sent for the battery of seventy-fives we had with us, and the four guns unlimbered in line right on the road. My company happened to be halted here and we were given a pretty exhibition by this artillery outfit, all young boys from France.

The range was soon found, then they started in. One, two, three, four, the guns would go, one after the other, almost as fast as a revolver, and over there, in the village, four dropping shells would explode, one, two, three, four. Those French kids were sending off about twenty shells to the minute, each dropping into the village. Smoke and dust were rising, walls crumbling, houses collapsing. We could see the villagers streaming out like ants, and taking up the hill above; it was reposeful to watch this. In about fifteen minutes, more than two hundred shells had been dropped into the village, and there was no more village.

"*Bien*," said the colonel, with heavy satisfaction. "Every time I've passed here, they've fired on my men. They won't fire any more. *C'est bien.*"

As we were marching along, we came to a Druse lying dead within our lines (my company was convoy guard at the moment, inside the cavalry and infantry frame). I saw a French soldier of the Tirailleurs go to the body and watched, curious to see if he were after possible loot. The old campaigner went to the body, slipped his toe under it, and gave it a little diagnostic heave. Instantly, he placed the muzzle of his rifle against it and shot. To my increasing surprise, the dead body immediately arched, and in convulsions, began to die all over again. With a second and a third shot, the tirailleur ended the agony.

The body lying there on our path had not been a dead body at all. It had been a live Druse playing possum, who had adopted this desperate method of getting within our lines to await a good chance to cut some one down. But he had not deceived the old campaigner's flair of that veteran French tirailleur.

It was all terrible work. The fighting which always takes place when the enemy is within your house, in your cellar, behind your apple tree; when the man who smiles at you in the daytime is likely to cut your throat at night. We were shooting our prisoners. Every civilian caught armed was shot. We pillaged and burned every village from which we were attacked or sniped. No doubt many innocents suffered with the guilty. There was no help for it: the French were in dire straits. And only the iron in them which caused them, with the enemy in their own back yards, still to thrust at his base, to attack him right in his own mountains as they had done at Mousseifré, at Rezzas and Suweida, and there seek a decision, was to save them.

Back we went, under fire to the very gates of Damascus.

We were looking forward to passing Christmas here and feasting a little, when orders came to march to Chuba, thirteen kilometers southeast of Damascus, to build and occupy a post there, and off we went with a *groupe mobile*.

It was the same kind of march to which of late we had become accustomed. Fired on all the way; rapine, murder and sudden death. The farm-house we chose for the post at Chuba was a fine building, almost a mansion. We had no sooner arrived than the Vingt-neuvième was at its old toils. First unpacking the mules, bringing in the *matériel*, the ammunition, the stores. Then tearing down walls and building others. The court was too large to be defended by a body as small as ours—we were down to about sixty men now. So while half of us tore down the old walls, half of us were putting them up again inside of the old circumference. All outhouses which might be used by a determined enemy were torn down. The outhouses near the main building were fortified into redoubts. We slept in these and made our *créneaux*, our loopholes, each man at the head of his bed. Our light piece of artillery, a mountain gun served by Malagasy from Madagascar, was set up in the court. We tore down neighboring houses for wood. They were built of a sort of clay mud reinforced by long poles. We piled the poles in our cellar, tons of them. The *groupe mobile* which had escorted us was made up mostly of Senegalese. We called them *gobis*. We saw that the *gobis* did their share. They worked hard, the *gobis*. At that they were always cold, the poor blacks.

They left us on the second day, and we toiled on. The Druses brought down a plane near by. We dragged it into the court. There was always work to do. Always new walls to be built, if there was nothing else. We built a platform on a roof on which a sentinel always stood with binoculars—each man two hours on, four hours off. Fleury, my little partner of Mousseifré, was one of these. There were four guards below, one at each redoubt. Plenty of guard duty.

Our job was to stop caravans as they passed, and search them for weapons, which constantly were being smuggled into Damascus. The special guard for this stuck its long bayonets into every sack. Out in front was a stream; we washed our clothes there. We were always washing because the post was crawling with what, in the World War, the French called *to-to's* and the Americans cooties. Once a week we would stand naked outside and boil in a caldron everything we wore. On guard duty we were scratching all the time.

Christmas came. We worked from five in the morning to six at night, upon which we had our Christmas dinner—a little fried beef, potatoes, water-cress and a little chocolate.

Then we settled to the miserable monotony of garrison duty in an isolated post. Supplies came to us twice a month; the convoy would have to fight its way to us; we were practically cut off. It rained continuously, it was cold; we stood guard in our capotes, wrapped in blankets. It rained and it rained. Misery and monotony. Our clothes rotted on us. The only warm moment of the day would be at morning coffee, when they served us a ration of tafia—the powerful Martinique rum. Once a week a plane, hovering over us, dropped a mail bag in the court. We were cut off, we were isolated, we had no way to get drunk and forget our woes—and yet all of that time we could clearly see at night the lights of Damascus, only thirteen kilometers away.

One day the airplane dropped more mail than usual and we were told to clean up for a *prise d'armes*.

I did not know what a *prise d'armes* meant, but cleaned up with the others. We boiled out our shirts, we cleaned our uniforms, sewed on buttons, stopped rips, shined our shoes, polished our belts, rubbed our equipment, oiled our rifles. After *soupe* at ten, the sergeants looked us over as Legion sergeants will—rectifying this, pulling a belt around, arranging a lapel, twisting us about as a nurse does a small child. Finally we all stood before the captain, our capotes buttoned on the left side, our sashes outside, too splendid for anything.

We marched outside; we lined up by sections, two deep. The captain came out and took the regular position in front of us. We presented arms, went through the manual, then presented arms again. An orderly came out of the post with a little tray holding shining things, and stood by the captain.

The captain called the names of Lieutenant Vernon and Lieutenant Boissier.

They marched to within three paces of him, and saluted. Meanwhile we were all standing at the "present arms." The captain got out a paper and read citations for the two lieutenants. Then taking from the tray two croix de guerre, pinned them on their tunics and shook their hands.

Then he called out:

"Adjudant-Chef Tokar." (He was a Czecho-Slovak.)

"Sergent Falberana." (An Italian.)

"Sergent Krivitch." (A German.)

"Sergent Doudelet." (A Frenchman.)

There was a little pause between each call, as each man marched up to within three paces of the captain. Doudelet marched up, and then, "Clare!" the captain called.

I was standing there at present arms, thinking of nothing like that, and I almost dropped my gun. I felt the back of my neck grow hot. But I marched up, still at the "present," and joined the line of the three "*sous-offs*." The captain read their citations and pinned on them the crosses. He came to me, read my citation, and pinned the croix de guerre on my capote, then shook my hand.

I know what I will be asked by those of my friends who read this. They will say, "Did he kiss you?"

He did not. He shook my hand. They don't kiss for the croix de guerre. The *accolade*—which by the way is not quite like any Anglo-Saxon kiss—is reserved for the *médaille militaire* and the Legion of Honor.

The captain then made a little speech, in which he told us it was *très bien*, we had *bien travaillé*—done good work—and *continuez*. And we presented arms to the flag, while the bugles called *Aux Drapeaux*, and we were dismissed, the *corvées* for the rest of the day being reduced to a minimum.

I had been so confused that I had heard and understood little of my citation, nor what it was all about. Later it appeared in print in the little sheet of the *ordres du jour*, and I still have a copy of it.

CLARE, Gilbert, à la vingt-neuvième compagnie du Premier Etranger.

Légionnaire d'un calme et d'un sang-froid remarquables, au cours du combat de Ressaz le 7 octobre 1925, a fait l'admiration de tous, marchant debout sous les balles et tirant tranquillement, et indifférent, comme au stand. S'était fait déjà remarqué au combat de Mousseifré le 17 septembre 1925.

Which means something like this. That at the Rezzas fight I gained admiration by strolling upright under fire, meanwhile shooting tranquilly, as if at target practice, and that my conduct had already attracted attention at Mousseifré.

I couldn't remember doing exactly this, but was glad to read of it. And I'll admit that the little cross gained that day is now my best-prized possession.

We remained at the post of Chuba another miserable month after this little interlude. The command's idea of breaking the desperate monotony was to give us hours and hours of drill in battle formation. And finally we were relieved.

We knew the relieving column had started by the shooting over Damascus way, and we followed its slow progress by the same means. It fought all the way, from five in the morning till dark and when it arrived it was carrying dead and wounded. Its colonel had been shot transversely through the chest.

When we went out the next day, he asked to

be carried by Legionaires. Twelve volunteered, and up hill and down, making bridges for him to ford the streams, we bore him on a litter every step of the thirteen kilometers to Damascus. He was to die of his wound in France a few months later.

We abandoned the post at Chuba. We had baptized it Poste Poux—Cootie Post. When everything was out, we turned our little cannon on it, and blew Poste Poux to blazes.

CHAPTER XIV

AFTER the blowing up of Poste Poux, we found ourselves marched to another part which, if less populated, afforded us a life as monotonous and exhausting. This was Halwé, in the Grand Liban, forty-five kilometers from Damascus. It had been a British camp during the World War and we were sent there to build barracks. Here again we suffered with cold and harassing toil. We were up at the top of a hill, and water was at the bottom a kilometer away; the water *corvée* was a heavy one. We were in rain, in sleet, in snow all of the time, and toiled with mud over our ankles.

One day, though, General Andrea passed by. He was the Andrea who had been colonel of the regiment of tirailleurs which had saved us at Mousseifré. While we stood about at the top of the hill, he addressed the *garde d'honneur* below. When he had gone and they had come up, they told us what he had said.

"*Légionnaires*," he had said, "we are about to

make a new little promenade in the country you know so well, the mountains of the Druses. We are going up to Suweida again, to take it for good this time. I saw you fight at Mousseifré, and I have asked that you come along in my column. So you are going to have a good time pretty soon."

We were delighted. We talked of nothing else for three days, for we were well fed up, it may be believed, with "the gardens of Damascus." And sure enough, a little while later appeared a regiment of Metropolitan infantry to take our place. We had built them fine barracks, we left them a post all in order and immaculately clean. The winter had gone, spring was on the way: they would have an easy time. But it was we who considered ourselves lucky now.

Two days later the Vingt-neuvième was on a train climbing up into our old country. A few kilometers from Ezraa, the train stopped and we got out with all our *matériel*.

The village of Khabish, inhabited by Maronites, or Christians, was a few miles away. Most of the company was sent up there to protect it. But my section was held at the little railroad station to defend that.

This was a fine place. We fortified it and unloaded for our personal use from the train thirty cases of grenades and enough rifle ammunition for a regiment. We built a platform on the flat roof where a man could stand guard in a chair, searching the country with his binoculars. Our new *adjudant-chef*, Stroh, was a fine fellow. He explained to us that, as trains passed all the time, we must keep ourselves immaculately clean, but that outside of that, and standing guard and the *corvées* of wood and water, which were easy ones here, we would have nothing to do.

We washed our clothes nearly every day, were spick and span and lived a fine life.

The Legion, however, was still the Legion. There was a Greek who had a canteen in Khabish, and had the unlucky idea of leaving some of his stores locked in the station store-room. The Legion flair brought several of our men to the door, the Legion ingenuity showed them how to pick the lock, and a case of cherry brandy, one of cognac, and one of beer were extracted.

That night, upstairs where we slept, Stroh, the *adjudant-chef*, was lecturing us for our conduct, the gist of his reflection being that he did not care how much we got drunk when off duty, but he was not going to have it on duty, when two tough old Legionaires who had missed the *rapport*, came staggering up and in, quite belligerent, and we had an example of our new adjutant's coolness and nerve. The men, one of them a Luxembourgeois, the other a Frenchman, were surly and threatening. The Luxembourgeois started to tell Stroh what he would do with him if he had his gun. Upon which Stroh instantly presented him with his own automatic, and said, "Let's see what you will do." And upon the man's doing nothing, put him to bed himself, as gently as a nurse.

Nearly every night the Maronite village would be attacked by the Druses, and every night, somewhere between us and Ezraa, the track would be cut. But we had nothing to do with that; we stayed with our station.

One night, five of us returning from a few hours' leave found a train stopped before the station, and every one on the qui vive, armed and ready.

It seemed that down the track a few kilometers three thousand Druses from the Grand Liban were crossing—men, women, children, cattle and all—to join the Jebel Druses in their mountains. We remained on the *alerte* all night but were not attacked.

The next day bands of *Partisans* were sent out to harass them. The *Partisans* were tribesmen friendly to the French. They followed the migrating people all day, returned with 2,000 sheep, and delivered to the captain, *officier de renseignements* who advised them, forty Druse heads, for which he duly paid them at the official rate of two hundred and forty francs a head—about seven dollars, the franc being then low.

Only the *Partisans* were thus rewarded. Regular troops got nothing. As Delaporte said, envious and indignant, his eyes sticking out at the proceedings, "We, we don't get even ten sous a head; we don't get anything! That's the way they treat the Legion!"

We were moved to Ezraa, to join the *groupe mobile* which was being formed for the new expedition on Suweida—which the Druses had reoccupied and refortified. We spent a week drilling with new marvelous automatic guns which had been furnished us, three to each section—drilling and going wild in the canteens.

It was here I went through a little adventure characteristic of the Legion. I had gone into a canteen with Van Lage, a German who had enlisted under this Dutch name. It is the rule that a private must leave the canteen to the "*sous-offs*," the non-coms, after eight o'clock. Eight o'clock came, the common soldiers left, but Van Lage and I, enjoying ourselves, remained. After a while the adjutant of our machine-gun company began to hint that we should go, and when we paid no attention to that, to order us to get out. We defied him, upon which he jumped to threats, roaring that he would throw us out. Following the conventional course of such repartee, we of course challenged him to come and try it. He did. In a minute we two were fighting seven or eight non-coms. I used my fists and we gave a good account of ourselves. The machine-gun adjutant's nose was bleeding, one eye blackened, the blood was spoiling his uniform. But after a while numbers began to tell. Rallying, the "*sous-offs*" picked us up bodily, and threw us outside on our heads.

But we were in no condition to be thus easily satisfied. We charged in again. Again they picked us up and threw us out. We insisted, and for a third time landed out in the road on our heads. But we were indomitable. In we went again.

I don't know how long this would have lasted, if a patrol of spahis had not come along with their sergeant. I happened to know the sergeant, which was good for us. He finally prevailed upon us to go home—and home we went, between four bayonets. The situation looked serious, but when he had us at the gate, he let us go.

The situation was still serious, however, for we had missed several *appels*, and had struck (struck is a mild term for it) officers, a serious offense in the Legion, one which made us subject to a court-martial. However, that machine-gun adjutant was a square lad. He knew he had been not quite sober, and that his methods had not been quite formal. So, although his fine uniform had been completely spoiled, he lodged no complaint; instead he came to us and said, now that we were about to go out on a new campaign, it would be better to start out with no grudges. But some of our own sergeants had been there during the fight, and though taking no part in it had witnessed it with interest. Our attitudes as we went out and lit on our heads had seemed the height of the comic to them, and it was often, for some days, they kidded us about it.

It was while in Ezraa that I first became acquainted with John Harvey.

Men of my company kept telling me that there was in the squadron of the Legion cavalry an Englishman, and that he had asked to see me. So one day I went over.

He was a Welshman from Cardiff, of medium height, broad shoulders, brown hair, gray eyes. His hands were still marked with the coal powder which had entered the pores when he worked in the mines as a boy. During the War he had been with the First South Wales Borderers and, at Ypres, had been struck in the head by a small splinter of shell.

At the time I met him, he was *ordonnance* to an officer—what in our army is a "striker" or, more popularly, a "dog-robber." This gave him special privileges and what was still more important, extra supplies of such delicacies as butter, canned milk, coffee and sugar.

So we sat in his tent and talked over coffee and bread and butter. Talked in the usual Legion talk. The Legionaire, like the old Napoleonic "grognard," is always kicking. A day seldom passes but he threatens to go off *en promenade*. But there was in Harvey's talk something more than that. He seemed heartily fed up with the Legion, and moody over what he considered wrongs. And his talk was more specific than the usual chatter of the kind from the fact that it had, it might be said, a geographical tinge. He spoke of the Syrian frontier to the south, of the English Transjordania beyond.

I went there again, several times, and met in his tent two Germans, Weisser and Lass.

Weisser had fought in the infantry during the World War and had been wounded. A Senegalese, charging a trench, had struck him with his big "coupe-coupe," and he still bore the long scar of it across the forehead. Now he was fighting side by side with the *gobis*. Lass had been in the German navy during the War. Since that he had spent two years in China and spoke some English.

It seemed nice to talk in English. And also to drink coffee and eat bread and butter! I went to Harvey's tent several times while in Ezraa.

Then the *groupe mobile* marched out of Ezraa toward Suweida, our old friend. This was to be quite an ambitious effort and another column, starting from Dera, toward the Transjordanian frontier, was to move on the Druse stronghold from the south, while ours attacked from the north.

The first night we camped at Mousseifré. Remnants of our old walls were still there, and I kicked a skull out of the soil, grim remnant of our stay here when a *bleu* in my first battle. The village was now pacified and was flying white flags. Going on, our company camped the next night on the very crest of Tel Hadie. We could see Suweida, across the valley, swarming with Druses putting up breastworks of stones.

At six o'clock the next morning, we marched on to the attack of Suweida, about six kilometers away. The Legion was the advance guard. It was a beautiful April morning, and for about twenty minutes we went unmolested across the plain. We could guess, more than we could see, the Druses massed on the slopes behind stones, stone hedges and inside the little blockhouses they had built. Suddenly from one of these blockhouses came a single shot, as if a signal. And a moment later a heavy fire poured upon us from all sides.

Our battalion moved slowly up the slope, dislodging the Druses from behind the rocks and walls, reducing one after the other the little blockhouses. It was a fight rather by sections than by companies, each section doing the best it could with its particular problem. It was a mopping-up proposition, with special care given that nothing alive should be left behind us. We were using hand grenades a good deal, and whenever halted, would put on our rifles the big *tromblon* attachment and fire the heavy rifle grenades which tore up the ground almost like shells. The Druses, retreating, would leap back from wall to wall. It was only during these bounds we would see them, and then it was our new automatics would do marvels, picking the flying bodies right out of the air.

To our right was a detachment of Algerian tirailleurs with a machine-gun. A little squadron of Druses charged them on horseback with sabers, and to our astonishment we saw the tirailleurs let it go and scatter. One of our squads drove off the Druses, recaptured the machine-gun and went on with it. Later, we took it back to the tirailleurs' headquarters, asking them innocently if they had not lost it—which raised quite a pother in that outfit.

On we went, from rock to rock, from wall

to wall. My company, which in Damascus had been down to sixty men from its original one hundred and thirty, had been refilled for this expedition. All the men in my squad were new now, except Budney, who as usual fought at my right.

Near the top a big blockhouse held us up for a time. The seventy-fives were signaled. They dropped a shell on the roof. Out the occupants scattered like chickens, while we picked them off with the automatics and rifle grenades.

The last few hundred yards we took in a charge at the bayonet. Up through green orchards we went yelling like fiends. And gaining the rim of the town, intrenched in a ditch along the road, to hold off the counter-attacks as the rest of the column came in.

At the same time the column from the south was coming in from its side. It had been severely cut up; the Druses had once reached its convoy, and the Senegalese guard had used its "coupe-coupes"; as they marched in they bore along with them their own dead.

Thus it was we took Suweida for the last time.

CHAPTER XV

WHEN the tricolor was flown over the recaptured citadel of Suweida that afternoon, it was the flag which our battalion carried which was run up, in honor of the fight we had put up that day. And for the third time since I had joined my company, it was cited in the orders of the army.

My company had built our camp on the left side, or exposed side of the town. The Druses were shooting at it and we could not sleep. So in a rage Budney and I got up to the wall and started firing away in return. A roar of our lieutenant stopped us. What in blankety blank blank did we mean by firing thus without orders? Let the machine-guns take care of this. The machine-guns did, all night, and we had little sleep.

Now began a series of small events which, I see it now, gradually worked me up toward the unlucky decision of which you will read somewhere at the end of this chapter.

The next day we had to bury our dead. Two

men from each squad of the entire column were told off for this detail, and I was one of the two from my squad.

This, reverential as we tried to make it, proved a terrible task, in this climate where the flesh quickly dissolves.

The place for the cemetery was behind the citadel. It was in rocky ground, the labor of digging proved terrible. The Legion honors its dead by digging its graves five feet deep. We toiled with pick and shovel that day from dawn till well in the afternoon.

Then the camions began to arrive, laden with the dead, coming up the hill under the spent bullets of distant Druse snipers. They lay there in the camions close, packed like cord wood, Legionaires, Tirailleurs, Spahis, Senegalese. As each camion arrived, a sergeant going into it with a man, passed the bodies one by one out to us, while we laid them on the ground side by side. There were about four hundred dead finally, laid in a motionless and gruesome line.

An officer of *renseignements* went along the line to register each man and collect the papers, the small objects, the trinkets upon him. The details of each outfit accompanied the officer to pick out their own by their uniforms, or the shreds that were left of them.

General Andrea now appeared with his staff, and a guard of honor from each outfit. Again we moved the dead, laying each by the side of his grave. The graves of the Tirailleurs and Senegalese were shallow; even cuffs and blows from their officers could not make them do even this task properly. But the grave of each Legionaire was five feet deep.

Two priests who were with the column now celebrated the Catholic burial service, and eight Mohammedans chanted in Arabic the services for the Tirailleurs and the Senegalese.

We then lowered the dead into their graves. My work was to go into each grave and receive from the others of my detail each body as it was handed down to me.

We then filled the graves. The arms of each dead Legionaire were crossed over his chest. We laid big stones upon him so that his remains might be less easily disturbed by the jackals and the Druses. With our hands—they don't throw dirt on a dead Legionaire—we smoothed earth between the stones. Only when the body was thus covered was more earth gently thrown in. On top we again placed great stones, and a line of smaller stones outlined the grave. Within the next few days, we made headstones for each, engraved with the name of the dead man, the date and place where he had fallen, and the traditional and fine phrase, *Tombé devant l'ennemi.*

General Andrea then made a speech. "The last time we buried our dead here the Druses dug them up again and scattered their remains to the wind. I promise you now that those just buried here will rest in peace. We are back in Suweida forever; our dead will never again be alone."

He saluted, the bugles blew *Aux Drapeaux*, and the details marched about the square at present arms, eyes left.

The next morning we changed camp, which meant we had to build walls. The Druses were sniping at us, and my squad sergeant, Budney and I were at the walls with a pair of binoculars, trymg to spy them out. They were in the sun, they were locating us by the flash made by the glasses, so my sergeant told me to get stones to make the wall higher here and build a *créneau.* I went out to a pile of stones outside, stooped, and just then from not more than a hundred yards, a flock of bullets passed just a few inches above the middle of my back. My bending to pick up a stone had been timed by the fates just exactly in time to save my life. A German behind me was not so lucky, receiving several shots in the stomach. And Demoulin, a Belgian, fell at the same time with a wound in the neck. I saw that the German was dead and went to Demoulin. "Give me a cigarette," he said, "it isn't bad. Just lots of blood, that's all." Though it looked like a terrible wound he proved a good diagnostician. That very day he was taken to Damascus by plane, and later recovered.

But Lieutenant Delaplane of the machine-gun section had also been struck by the same discharge a little farther up the hill, and we found him dying. He had been a great favorite with the men. In action he would walk alongside of us with just his stick, chatting with us freely, making nothing of his rank. We saw now that he was going fast; he had been fairly riddled with bullets.

General Andrea, notified, came hurrying on his horse, dismounted, kneeled by the dying man, and pinned on him his own croix de guerre.

This was about the last of the fighting. Next day our camp was moved once more, this time to the western side of the town, which was less exposed. But now the backbone of the Druse rebellion had been broken. Every day groups came in with white flags to lay their submission before General Andrea. The French were eager to pacify the land, and their terms were easy. Each tribesman submitting must turn in his rifle and pay one Turkish pound. Cheap for one and a half years of such fighting as they had given themselves! In a little while the surrounding region was as peaceful as a windless lake; we could go into the orchards and groves, stop at the fountains with no fear of a sniper's bullet, or of having our throat cut by some crawling wild man.

Now began the monotony and boresome toil which was to drive me mad. We had been moved to the center of town for *repos*. We soon found what this *repos* was to be. First we were put to building huge bakery ovens for the column.

In the Legion men of all trades can be found. For whatever there is to be done, you can find some one who knows how to do it. But with many of my comrades, of building ovens I knew nothing. We could bring stones for the masons, however. At bringing in the stones we were put.

This did not mean steam-shovels and cranes,

nor trams nor trucks. It meant bringing in great stones individually one by one on your shoulder. It meant digging each out of the earth, heaving it to the shoulder, and staggering across rough ground with it. And doing this over and over again, over and over again, and then again. And always in a broiling sun.

I was seeing Harvey quite often now—either in tent at the cavalry quarters, or in the canteen, over a bottle of wine. He often had Weisser and Lass with him. He was discontented and moody. And the two Germans were suffering with heimweh. All the men of the Legion when things go badly will speak of "taking a promenade" but usually this is only talk. At first I think we talked as did all the rest, without any real intentions. But little by little—I don't remember how—the project was taking more definite shape in our minds.

One thing which served to tempt me was a map Harvey showed at times. He was a lieutenant's orderly, and he had access to this lieutenant's map. He would spread it out in his tent, and we would pore over it. Over there, south, a little beyond Bosra was the frontier. Suweida showed as only some forty kilometers north of this line between Syria and Transjordania which was under British mandate. Over across there was Freedom, respite from this heavy labor, this desperate monotony. And a chance perhaps to return home. Since I had been in the Legion I had not allowed myself to think of home for a single minute. It was only by keeping your mind at neutral you could bear the knowledge that you were in for five years. But now, whenever I looked at that map, I thought of home. And it did seem just a tiny little jump from Suweida across the border, to freedom. Over there were the British; they never sent back any foreign Legionaire. Forty kilometers. Hardly more than a day's march. Or, allowing for detours and roughness of country, since we could not fly, two days at the most. A little luck, two days' walking—and there we'd be—out of the Legion—free.

However, nothing was determined yet. We toiled on at the bakery. That was finished at last. Then, without respite, we were started at rebuilding the citadel.

This was the citadel which we had blown up less than a year before. Now we were to rebuild it. It was a great building four stories high.

I saw myself carrying stones for month upon month, month upon month.

But that was not all. The land was now in complete peace. You could go out upon the plain and pick poppies and daisies if you wished. And all kinds of projects were in the air. Suweida was to regain the beauty it had possessed before the revolt had begun. The railroad was to be extended from Bosra. I knew now at what they used the Legion in peace time. After the bakery, the citadel; after the citadel it would be something else. I had still almost four years of my enlistment to run. I saw the four years stretching before me, an eternity of carrying stones on my back, like a fellah, like the slaves who built the Pyramids. When I saw we were to rebuild the citadel, I became all revolt. And there was Harvey's map with its wonderful promise ever under our nose.

It was about that time I saw George Seldes, the American correspondent. I was in the canteen, talking to Harvey, when I was told the lieutenant wanted me. I went over. Seldes had been told there was an American in the company and had asked to see me.

He had flown over from Damascus and was going back: he had little time to give me. We passed a few words, then he said good-by and good luck.

But from the hill a little while later I saw his plane winging away. How free he was!

I was fed up. I remembered General Andrea's words when in Damascus he had promised us this "little promenade" to Suweida. This was the promenade. Toiling like a slave under a broiling sun day after day. I was fed up; a monstrous *cafard* had hold of me. I now resolutely entered into Harvey's scheme. He had been of this mind from the first, and several times had declared that if we did not go—Weisser, Lass and I—he would start alone.

Circumstances favored us. I received a prize of twenty-five francs for my shooting at Mousseifré and at Rezzas. This sum, so it was decided in one of the conferences we were having more and more often, would finance us. Cached in Harvey's *musettes* in his tent were stores we had gradually accumulated—canned sardines and pork, cigarettes, a small bottle of cognac, two *bidons* full of coffee.

Where we were troubled was about arms. Had

there been fighting, we would have had our rifles of course. As it was, every day, while we worked, the rifles would be placed in a stack in the middle of the street and under guard. I decided that it would be impossible to get my rifle without awakening suspicion, and so did Weisser and Lass. On the other hand, Harvey, who as orderly shared none of our deadly toil, always had his *mousqueton*, his carbine. We decided that this would have to do us. It must be understood that our projected flight was to be through a country lately hostile, and even now half desert, crossed by marauding Bedouins, and where settled, settled with villages where one was very apt to have one's throat cut.

One morning General Gamelin arrived in a plane and reviewed us. We dressed up, paraded. He made a speech; the band played "C'est le général qui passe," and at eleven o'clock we were dismissed *en fête* for the day. I don't think any gentle irony entered into our decision, but there and then we decided this was the day.

So after the *soupe* I went to Harvey's tent. Down the hill were the gardens of what had been the Sultan's summer palace, and in these was a cistern with beautiful, clear, cool water. Taking all of our clothes as though we were going to engage in a big wash, and incidentally our *musettes*, our *bidons*, two of which were already filled with sweetened coffee, and taking along still more carelessly the *mousqueton*, Harvey and I went down to these gardens and the cistern.

Here, after an hour, Weisser and Lass joined us, also with all their clothes and their *bidons*. We filled the empty *bidons* with the clear cold water, and then started to wash our clothes.

Other men from other outfits were here also, washing their clothes, and our plan demanded that we outstay them. So we washed leisurely, taking as much time as we could, and washed all the things we had that could be washed, hung them about to dry, and if they dried too soon, found some speck of dirt about them somewhere and washed them over again. It was pleasant and cool down there, among the trees, by the cool water; the other men jested with us. For the time the military life we had grown to loathe took on a pleasant tinge, and Weisser began to get uneasy and fearful.

We had outstayed every one by this time, it had grown dark, we had missed the assembly at six. We told Weisser to leave if he wanted to, that we were going through with it, and he finally decided to stick.

Night had come. We crept into a little room in the front of the palace ruins, opened a can of sardines, ate the contents with some biscuits, smoked a cigarette and were ready. We opened the door on the outside, and far off in the night we could see the winking signals of Ezraa, Bosra and Mousseifré. Studying the map, we had decided we should pass between Bosra and Mousseifré on our way southwest to the little village of El Umtaye, which, on the map, was shown as across the frontier, and in Transjordania.

So orienting myself, I took the lead and stepped out.

CHAPTER XVI

STEPPING out of that little side door of the Sultan's palace, we could see the blinker lamps of the distant posts at Bosra and Mousseifré winking in the night. Bosra, almost due south, and no more than ten kilometers from the border, was in the direction we wanted. But stopping at Bosra was a branch railroad that came down from the west. I saw that if we held a little to the right of Bosra, it would bring us across this railway. That would help us both as to distance and to direction when we got down there. The thing to do, then, was to hold a little to the right of Bosra's winking light, and well to the left of Mousseifré's.

We now gathered up everything, left the shadow of the building and set off down the hill. The night was moonless but full of bright stars. We crept carefully, for we were still near the sentinels. Right here I began to realize something of which I had not thought. My three chosen companions were cavalrymen, unused to tramping and awkward of foot.

We had to climb over a succession of stone hedges and walls as we slid down the hill. My companions were making an unholy racket at it. Finally Harvey, scrambling, knocked over an entire wall; in separate stones it went hurtling and clattering down the slope. We froze, our hearts in our mouths, expecting every moment the rattle of a machine-gun. But the sentinels had already degenerated in these weeks of peace. No alarm was given, nothing stirred.

We went on, more carefully, after a time, and finally reached the bottom of the hill and the open country. Aiming a little to the left of Bosra's light, we cut across the land.

For a while everything went well and we made good progress. The way was up and down, in loose rock; hard going, but the night was cool. But soon my cavalrymen began to lag. I was hardened to footing it over such country; they had seen it only from the saddle and were soft. They wanted to stop all of the time and rest. My idea was that we should march infantry style—fifty minutes at a time with ten minutes' rest between.

Harvey began to argue about the direction. I knew that Bosra was in the direction we wanted, and that by keeping just a little to the right of it, we would cross the branch railroad when we neared the border. Harvey kept arguing that I was leading too far to the left, that we should steer farther to the right. The two Germans—Lass spoke English, but Weisser spoke none—though puzzled at our discussions, and reluctant to decide between us, naturally sided with Harvey. So time and time again, against my arguments, which I did not like to push too far for fear of disrupting the party, we slanted a little farther to the right.

Finally, as dawn was coming, we stopped in the lee of a pile of rocks, for it had been decided we should march only at night.

The light came slowly; we were keenly trying to make out where we were. As the light grew, I began to get more and more strongly a strange feeling that I knew this land. We were at the top of a long slope. Down below, a village gradually showed up out of the shadows. The light grew, and suddenly I knew where we were. That village down there was Mousseifré! We were on the very slope down which, a few months ago, the Druses had poured in their charge on our little wall fort!

And Mousseifré, of course, was much too far to the right and to the north. We had done much useless tramping. Still, getting out the map, we saw that we had nevertheless made fair progress and were now only about twenty kilometers from the border. The map showed a small village called El Umtaye, due south from us, just over the frontier. We decided we would make for El Umtaye. There would be some English post there, we felt sure, and some English intelligence officer to whom we could surrender (the British returned to the French authorities only those deserters who were French). The way would take us across the branch railroad from there, which ran about five kilometers inside the boundary line, and the Bosra light would still be our guide.

We did not know that the map was wrong as to El Umtaye or that the boundary line had been rectified since the making of it. And that El Umtaye now squatted just inside the line, on the French side!

We broached our provisions and had breakfast. We were still holding to our plan of marching by night and hiding by day.

After a while, as the sun rose, villagers came

out into the fields to the right and the left, and began to plow the ground with their wooden plows, behind their lean, long-legged oxen. The rocks hid us on one side, but not on the other. As the morning wore on, more and more peasants came out into the small fields among the rocks, and we grew more and more uneasy.

Finally we decided this would not do. Ahead of us was a big pile of rocks that promised better refuge. Taking up our gun and our *bidons*, we walked across to this pile. We found it gave us good cover, a sort of cave, and settled there for the day.

We were so far pretty well pleased with ourselves and the arguments of the night ceased. We lay in our cave, cool in the heat of the day, dozed, ate and drank. We ate indeed too much—consuming all of our provisions. One more night's march, we thought, and we are there. And there'll be no trouble about provisioning once arrived at El Umtaye.

We even discussed what we would do when we got across. Harvey spoke glowingly of the British-officered patrol service over there. You rode swift camels. When you had finished your patrol, you slept in barracks. It was like being a mounted policeman; it was a cushy job. We might be able to enlist in that, and save up to get home.

When darkness had come, and all the posts were again winking to each other in the night, we picked out the Bosra light and started again, laying our course a little to the right of it.

For a time everything went well, though the going was hard, through loose rock, up and down, and those soft cavalrymen were suffering and lagged far behind the pace I would have liked to take. We often climbed hedges to pass through small wheat fields. Whenever we neared a village, the howls of dogs warned us, and we circled around. There was a slight film in the sky, and the night was pitch-dark.

We lost the Bosra light behind a rise. When we picked it up again there was some question as to whether that was it. Harvey again began to argue that we should go off more to the right.

We had tramped hours now and felt we should be getting to the railroad track. "It must be just a little ahead," we would say, and march farther and still not come to it. "Where in hell *is* that railroad?" we began to ask querulously. Every now and then we'd think we were seeing an embankment ahead, and then it would prove to be just a hill. "Good God," we began to say, "we should have passed it hours ago!" We were out of food, our *bidons* were empty. Still we walked, and still we did not come to the railroad. Harvey began to say that I had lost the way.

He was moody and of flaring temper. I began to wish I had taken my rifle with me. With it I think I should have gone on my way alone, as these constant bickerings about direction were exhausting, and apt to end fatally. But Harvey had the only gun in the outfit, and this was no country to be tramping unarmed, what with its roving bandits, its fortified villages peopled with doubtful characters. Besides I felt sorry for the two Jerries, who, between us, were puzzled and nonplussed.

As a matter of fact, the light we had taken lately for that of Bosra was that of a small post, not on the map and a bit to the left of Bosra's blinker, which was not showing at the time. Still we tramped, still we cursed and longed for a railroad, still we didn't come to it. Then we topped a rise, descended—and found ourselves right in front of Bosra. Christ, its blinker was winking right over our heads; we were right under it!

This was not any place where we wanted to be at all. Bosra! We lay quiet awhile, then started circling it far to the right. The situation now had one advantage; we knew exactly where we were. From Bosra the branch railway went west toward the main line; if we crossed the line at right angles, we would be going in the right direction. And we were only some five kilometers from the frontier!

But as we stumbled along in the night, giving Bosra and its garrison a wide berth, Harvey started raving again. It was all my fault, it seemed; we should have been across long ago. "How the blankety blank and black regions," I answered, "could I help it if the whole blankety land was full of blankety posts winking their blank, blank blinkers?" And so we went like boys on a camping trip that is going wrong.

Meanwhile we were having trouble finding the railroad. Our plan had been to circle Bosra wide, and cross it above. We must be circling too wide; time was passing; we tramped and tramped and came to no railroad.

Finally we did. Here was the railway at last. We crossed it, we sighted the direction we should take to cut the frontier line in the dark. On we went, dragging our heavy feet. There was no light now to give us direction. Over there in Transjordania, no little friendly winks to lead us. We stumbled along in the dark trying to hold the right direction. Soon Harvey and I were disagreeing again. He wanted to swing to the right, I to the left. And thus discussing, suddenly we came to the railroad! We had made a circle in the dark; we were back where we had started!

We figured our direction once more, and made a new start. We tramped on for an hour and suddenly—there was the railroad again! Harvey was once more raving.

"All right," I said,—I felt by now that our only chance lay in keeping our heads,—"let's start again, and you lead the way this time."

So we sallied once more for the frontier,—it was so near, too!—following in the footsteps of Harvey, who went first, carbine in hand.

Within ten minutes, we were at the railway again. We were bewitched!

"Hell! We are lost!" we admitted now. We

were by this time utterly worn out, our nerves on edge, and we knew we were lost. The night was beginning to lift. We walked into a wheat field and lay down.

We slept a little. We were cold, we had no food, our *bidons* were empty. But all was not lost. We were surely very near the frontier. By studying the way in daylight, we'd be able to make it the next night.

When dawn came we were stiff and weak. A little way off I saw a stream, and we filled our *bidons* and returned into the wheat.

As the light increased I was getting my bearings, and finally I could see, a little way back of us, the telegraph poles of a railroad line—the one we had passed so many times last night. There it stretched out so very far, north of us. Then, our way lay in the opposite direction.

I told the others of my discovery, and we got into serious dissension. I felt certain of where we were now. I was for sticking strictly to our original plan of hiding in the daytime. The wheat field in which we lay was an ideal hiding place. I thought we should remain here all day, get our bearings at sunset, and start out at dark, taking some star as guide. I felt that this was our only chance, that any other course meant disaster.

But Harvey by that time was disgusted, stubborn and mad. "We have no food," he argued.

"I've often gone two days without food in the Legion," I said. "What's a day without food?" I was getting wild with contempt for the softened dog-robber.

He argued that we were only a few kilometers from the boundary at the most, that a dash would make it, and he was going to make that dash right away, too, and not waste time in a bleeding wheat field. I could stay if I wanted to. He was going.

In spite of my forebodings, seeing that Weisser and Lass were with him, I said, "All right. Go ahead, then, I'll go too. We'll stick together."

So we started out in full daylight. But we had not gone more than a little way when we disagreed over the direction once more. And this time we parted. "You go your way and I'll go mine," I said.

So we parted, going off in different directions like school boys in a huff, Weisser and Lass following him hesitantly.

In a few minutes, I saw Harvey making wild signals to me to come back. They had come across a friendly villager, who had dates and bread. We bought some of these from him, and feasted there by the side of the camel path. Harvey spoke a few words of Arabic. With these and gestures we managed to get some information from the Bedouin. He showed us the way toward El Umtaye, which our map showed as being on the Transjordanian side of the border.

So we set out again, refreshed, hopeful once more, though I was still wishing we had hidden till night. We made such a strange group, one so apt to draw attention, we four weary men in uniform, carrying a rifle.

We had been going on for about an hour and a half, when suddenly El Umtaye came into view, a walled village on a crest. Not so far ahead, it spelled final success and freedom.

We were going along a camel path then, and passed a lot of villagers at harvest. They seemed to pay no attention to us; they kept on working as we passed. But I could see their lowering glances taking us in sideways. We went on a little further, and heard a shout behind us.

A great big black-bearded Bedouin horseman

was coming toward us at the trot of his white mare. He carried a slung Mauser rifle, and bandoliers of cartridges crossed on his chest. We stopped, as he got near. Harvey raised his carbine and ordered him to halt.

The black-bearded person reined up, made two or three big signs of the cross to show he was a Christian, then, smiling in a friendly way, dismounted and came toward us.

He seemed very friendly, his teeth flashed as he smiled, and Harvey let him come up. He offered us cigarettes; we began to smoke, and tried to chat, Harvey using his few words of Arabic, every one gesturing. He seemed to be offering us help to get across.

But there was something about him I did not like. His eyes kept going to Harvey's carbine. Also, he was edging closer and closer to Harvey, under cover of his attempts at small talk. I moved off a few feet to one side and watched him all ready. And suddenly I saw a telltale flash in his eye, and sprang.

The flash of his eye had preceded his action by a fraction of a second. He had leaped upon Harvey and had wrested the carbine from him. But I was only a fraction of a second behind.

Out of his grasp went the carbine, and into mine.

Backing up, he brought his Mauser down from its sling and started throwing a cartridge into the chamber. At the same time, backing up also, I was wrestling at the lock of my gun to throw a cartridge in. As I was doing so, going backward I stumbled over a stone, and flopped head over heels—just as his first shot went singing exactly through the space where I had stood just a fraction of a second before.

I was up in a trice, of course. He was running in a wide circle through the fields, shooting as he went, and on one knee I tried to pot him. He was yelling wild high-pitched yells, and looking over at the harvesters, we saw those peaceful-looking persons pulling long rifles out of the wheat. Then they came running fast in their flapping bloomers, along the ridges to our right and left, shooting as they went, yelling like jackals.

We took off down the camel path, still headed for El Umtaye. The Bedouins came on after us. Some, in their bare feet, were incredibly fast, streaking through the rocks and the wheat, trying to cut us off. I shot at the most threatening of these, halting their zeal. Our black-bearded friend, on his horse once more, was following at a respectful distance, rather directing than hungry for close contact. They were all yelling like fiends, and their bullets spattered the dust around us.

Pounding along in our heavy hobnailed shoes, panting, weary to death, we now luckily came upon a camel train carrying wheat toward the village. We got ahead of the camels, using them as a screen, and the pursuit seemingly ceased.

A half kilometer further, still running toward El Umtaye, which beckoned us on from the top of its ridge, we came upon another group of the charming inhabitants of the region. They made great gestures of friendship; they seemed to wish to help us get away. We stopped, though now less trustful than we had been.

They were very friendly, but they kept pressing closer and closer toward Harvey, who had the carbine once more. He sensed danger and started to back away, calling to them and motioning that they stand back. One stubborn fellow kept on pressing. "Keep back, keep back," Harvey roared, gesturing. Then as the fellow kept edging closer, he suddenly let him have it with the carbine right through the stomach, at four feet. Another sprang, and Harvey let this one have it right between the eyes, shattering his skull.

"Now we are cooked," we thought. "Now it's all off." A terrific uproar had arisen. Women came running from huts near by, threw themselves upon the dead, and began to send up howls of lamentation and yelps for vengeance to the sky. Once more we turned and ran, rifle bullets coming at us from all angles, the whole population in clamor. We ran and ran; we shook them off by close shooting, and were under the walls of El Umtaye at last.

The *caïd* and a group of villainous retainers aroused by the sound of shooting, had come out to meet us. They spoke a little English; they professed interest in our adventure, and willingness to help us.

But I noticed mutterings in the outskirts of the band, and villainous looks. I thought I saw several men toying with long knives under their garments. "Watch out," I murmured to Harvey.

I looked behind for a moment to see if our late pursuers were coming on, and when I turned back, Harvey was empty-handed, and the *caïd* had the carbine!

One thing can be said about Harvey. He may have been of hair-trigger temper and injudicious at times; but whenever we were in real trouble, he rose to it. He now sprang to the *caïd* and let him have it with both fists, right and left.

At the same time, the whole group jumped us, and in a moment we were in the whirl of a terrific hand-to-hand fight. I had been right about the knives. Every Bedouin now had one in hand—a long, curving, ugly thing.

The *caïd* was trying to throw a cartridge into the chamber of the rifle and Harvey, knowing there was none in the magazine, was laughing at him and at the same time crashing his fists into his face. Weisser and Lass, uttering great German curses, were carrying several men on their backs. As for me, I had been selected by a great horrible fellow armed with a long knife. His hair was braided into two long pigtails. His black eyes were bloodshot; and as he continuously crept toward me with the long knife ready, he snarled and stank like a jackal. I was holding him off by picking up great stones and hurling them into his face. Down I'd stoop, scoop up a stone and let him have it. But shaking it off, or dodging, he would come on, crouched like a hyena. I'd let him have another—and still he would come on, his long, curved, sharp knife ready for my throat.

But finally Harvey wrenched the carbine from the *caïd*, managed to get a cartridge in, and shot him through the leg, shattering the bone.

Out of El Umtaye all the inhabitants came pouring with knives, with scythes, with pistols, with rifles, and breaking loose we tore for it. Not for the frontier this time—we knew that only massacre and torture awaited us that way. But there was a little station I could see off to the right, a French station in French Syria. There might be a French post there—it was a matter now of saving our lives. So toward it we ran, the entire population now after us.

We had come out of the last fight in piteous condition. We had lost our *bidons* and our *musettes*, our kepis. The clothes had been literally torn off the backs of the two Germans, and I had badly twisted my ankle which in a trice had swelled to twice its size.

Our way was down a shallow dry watercourse with a ridge alongside. Behind us and along the ridge the pursuers were pouring, while bullets fairly rained about us from all sides. I had not gone far before one took a bit of the skin off my right ear. A moment later another neatly took off the heavy heel of one of my hob-nailed *brodequins*. As a nice Fate would have it, this was on the foot opposite to my sprained ankle. So as I ran each step was alternately on a sprained ankle, and on a heelless shoe.

Down the road, charging on his bare feet at incredible speed, came a wild man brandishing a medieval spear. I took Harvey's carbine, knelt, shot—and he vanished like the creature of a dream he looked.

We were now retreating Legion style, in *décrochage*. I would take the carbine for a while, and kneeling in the center of the path, would fight a rear-guard action, shooting very carefully—which was discouraging to the pursuers. Then I would run up to Harvey, Weisser and Lass, who meanwhile had gone on, and pass the carbine to Harvey. He in turn would kneel in the center of the path and hold them off while we went on; then would come running and pass the gun to Lass, who in his turn knelt in the path.

Little by little the hail of bullets which had rained about us as we left the village was thinning. Our careful shooting was taking effect. If they had been good shots, we would have been hit, of course, a hundred times over.

Still at the *décrochage* style, we were nearing the station, and as we neared, the pursuit lagged more and more. It was not our shooting alone which was the cause of this. If we had thought, the phenomenon would have made us suspicious of that little station, with its red roof, and of what it might hold.

Finally, with a last buzz of a last discharge, and a yowling of spent bullets, the pursuit ceased, and we found ourselves walking in complete quiet. The little railway station was quite near now. And we came to a water tank, a great concrete trough, filled with cool, wonderful water, and stopped, and put our heads into it like horses.

There was a little cover there. We hid. The rest of the day we spent by the cool water tank, drinking, smoking and resting. We were in despair, of course, at this catastrophe to our cherished plans. We were worn out and soul-sick.

But little by little, as time passed and everything remained quiet about us, we began to gather up a little courage once more.

Why could we not still do it? We knew the way now; bitterly we had learned it. There was the frontier, a few kilometers away. Why not take another chance and cut for it?

So just before sundown, we picked ourselves up, Harvey took up the carbine and, a forlorn and battered group, we set out.

We had not gone a hundred yards when from behind a stone wall, where he had been all the time, a mounted Syrian gendarme rode out and shot his pistol into the air.

We knew what that meant. The end. Harvey dropped his carbine; we all put our hands up and waited for the gendarme.

CHAPTER XVII

FROM the moment that shot of the Syrian gendarme made its little plop sound in the quiet of the desert, there by the little station near the border, my experience in the Legion entered a phase on which I don't like to think.

Yet the beginning was not bad at all. The Syrian gendarme was a good fellow, rather sorry he had had to catch us. He took us to the post, at the station, and we were well treated. The captain seemed to feel sorry for us. He asked us why the devil we had not crossed at night—which awakened a wound not very old. When evening came they even gave us a little feast. The *caïd* of the village of Taiyibie—not of El Umtaye!—came over with some of his retinue. We squatted around huge platters of mutton and rice, drank tea, smoked out of bubble pipes. The *caïd* had a robust sense of humor. He kept asking us why we did not hit our hosts across the neck and beat it; and the gendarmes roared at the joke, and we did, and had a good time. When night had come the gendarmes gave us their quilted sleeping-bags and we slept the sleep, perhaps not of the just, but of thoroughly exhausted deserters—which is still more profound. We were too tired to try to appreciate our situation, or to wonder what would be done with us.

In the morning, we were started to Deraa under guard of a corporal and three men. This did not prove so bad either. The gendarmes were on horseback, and we were afoot, but when the corporal noticed that I limped, he impressed a burro from one of the villages we passed, and I rode on that, my long legs touching the ground. After a while the corporal found more burros, and the three cavalrymen were also mounted. The corporal amused himself exchanging a few long shots with a bandit he knew on the way, which enlivened the journey, and he showed us the place where we should have crossed the frontier had we had any sense, which saddened us. And thus on our four burros we came into Deraa.

Here we were taken to the post of the gendarmerie, and questioned, all the details of our fight with the Bedouins being taken down—which caused us to remember that our adventure had not been without violence. We were then locked up in the guard-house of the barracks of the Syrian troops garrisoned there. The captain came to see us.

He was a little fat man. He greeted us with a volley of oaths and insults, *sacrés cochons* and so forth. You see, the Legion had always been rather indiscreet in its show of contempt for Syrian troops, and this touchy captain was getting even on the four Legionaires thus luckily placed in his power.

This captain, whose name I wish I could remember so as to deliver it to the infamy it deserves, kept gloating over us all the time we were there, coming in often under the excuse of questioning us. He hated specially Harvey and the Germans, and liked to declare to them that the British and the Germans were a band of *salopards*. Our food was good enough, but hardly sufficient. But one day, looking us over, he decided that we "were still too fat" and the ration was cut in half.

At last handcuffs—or thin chains, rather—were tied around our wrists, and chained two by two, we were taken to Damascus on the train.

Here we were imprisoned in the old Turkish

citadel, a structure dating back perhaps to the crusades. We were in one of the towers; there were no windows, and what light and air we got came in by the deep loopholes. The place had been partitioned into large cells. We were about thirty in mine, and it was stifling hot.

This prison was well peopled. It was crammed full with an Eastern population—Syrians, Arabs, Druses, Senegalese, Tunisians, Algerians, Moroccans, Turks and Frenchmen. The Legion was well represented; we found some thirty comrades there. One Syrian bandit told me with pride of the thirty gendarmes he had killed. He was a mere boy, just sixteen, and I saw him go away to be hanged in the public square before I left. The death cell by the doors was full of Syrians from Damascus, caught in the fighting in the "gardens." We passed them every day going in and out for exercise, and their cheerfulness always astounded us. Two other Syrians were serving hundred-year sentences for rebellion. We were thus in a place rather terribly eloquent of ruthless authority and iron-handed administration tempered with little mercy. We could not help being uneasy as to what would be dealt out to us by the Conseil de Guerre which was soon to try us.

The régime itself of the prison was not bad, though the food, what with the thin soup and the foul meat, was about uneatable, and the place crawled with vermin. I still had a little money and could get some chocolate which the cook would make for us. What saved us to some degree was the fact that early in the morning we were taken upon the roof, and remained there till five. Once a week we were taken down to the river which ran by the foot of the citadel, and washed our clothes. Once a week we had a hot shower.

The failure of our expedition had left its dissensions. Weisser and Lass were angry with Harvey. On the other hand I had made up with him. Lass would not speak to me because, having been given a few cigarettes, I had shared with Harvey and forgotten him. He was with some Germans at the time, and I thought he had cigarettes. It was one of those miserable quarrels typical of prison life.

Mostly we took our sleep during the day, on the roof. The vermin and the racket made by the gamblers made it impossible to sleep at night. In the big rooms within the partitions, the natives gambled every night, squatting in a big circle around the cards in candle-light. Nearly always the games ended in quarrels and in fights. Flop would go the cards in some one's face, the room in a moment would be a shrieking bedlam of struggling men, the gendarmes would storm in, their riding crops rising and falling, and finally order would be restored.

It was a black and anxious existence I was living when one day came a ray from the outside. The American consul in Damascus, Mr. Keeley, came to see me.

What had happened was this. George Seldes, the American newspaper correspondent whom I had seen at Suweida, hearing of my desertion and capture, had written an article which said I had been sentenced to be shot. This had been printed in the United States. And on the night of June 6, Mr. C. P. J. Mooney, editor of the "Commercial Appeal," of Memphis, had telephoned the news to my father at Biloxi—the first word, by the way, my father had had about me since I had vanished from my family's ken two years before.

Mr. Mooney—he is dead now—was a close friend of my father. The two men had immediately got busy with the wire, using all the influence they could muster in Washington. And the State Department had acted and notified Mr. Keeley.

So he had gone to see the general commanding the region. He did not know just what it was all about then; he rather fancied I had been shot already, and was prepared to ask for my body. The bluff old general was astonished. "*Mais non*, *mais non*, no American has been shot. *Mais non*, no one of that name has been shot. Besides, this is all foolishness—there was little probability, there was no probability that any one would be shot."

So it was not bad news Mr. Keeley brought. And he had word from my family, and the knowledge that far over there they were working for me. And more. He asked me if I needed anything. I did. A list was made out by Mr. Keeley's secretary who had come with him. And I feasted that night, as did many of my comrades.

After that Mr. Keeley came once or twice every week. And with him came each time a complete meal sent over from a Syrian restaurant near by—meats, potatoes, vegetables. Oh boy!

Meanwhile the date of the Conseil de Guerre was nearing, and we were discussing our chances a lot. One thing had been lifted from our shoulders. I had learned from Mr. Keeley that the killing of the several Bedouins in the frontier affray would not be on the calendar. The military authorities had declared immediately that they could not afford to countenance attacks upon men in uniform, and that our defense, deadly as it had proved, would not be brought up against us.

So we were hoping for the best. Weisser, always a pessimist and a bit sardonic of humor, railed at our optimism, but Harvey, the Welshman, was giving himself up to it entirely, and was speaking of a few months' sentence.

I did three days in the "cachot" with four sergeants, all of us having failed to salute the *sergent major* of the gendarmes up on the roof one morning. The dreaded cachot proved to be a joke. The wall rose only a few feet, and above that was just barbed wire. Our friends passed us reading matter, cigarettes, chocolate, even a bottle of brandy. We spent the time sleeping, eating, smoking; it was the best period I had in the citadel!

A few days before the Conseil de Guerre, the counsel appointed to defend me came to see me. He was an artillery captain, a thickset, swarthy Frenchman, and took his job conscientiously. He questioned me all over again, then advised me. His advice was to tell my story in an absolutely straightforward fashion, keeping precisely to the truth so that I could not be entangled in the questioning. He said that he would make his plea on two points—the fact that there was no fighting when I deserted, and the good record I had made before—and that he would throw me on the mercy of the court, asking for a light sentence with surcease (suspension of sentence). This all suited me well.

I can see now that I should have said I was drunk when I went over the hill. As a matter of fact I had done the thing in sobriety, not having had a drink for two days. But that would have been the explanation which would have satisfied and seemed simple to every one. That a Legionaire should get drunk and thus "take a promenade"—that was something comprehensible to every one.

Sergeant d'Etienne, who had left the Legion and was now a civilian, came to see me and also Sergeant Doudelet. They brought me food and clothes and talked with me a long time, and reassured me. They thought my sentence would be light.

Finally, on July 16, 1926, the four of us, plus Schop, an Austrian who had deserted on a venture of his own, were placed, chained two by two, in a black Maria drawn by mules and driven by a Senegalese, and through the streets of Damascus we went to the building where sat the Conseil de Guerre.

We were taken immediately to a small room upstairs and waited anxiously, seated on the hard benches, while the Conseil leisurely convened downstairs. A long wait and a nervous one. Finally, "Schop!"—the name was bawled downstairs, and a gendarme took the Austrian down.

He was down there a long time and came back looking worried. It seemed that they had asked him a terrible lot of questions. Also they had accused him of having deserted with ammunition—which he had not, he said. This for a moment lowered Harvey's optimism. "I suppose they'll make some fuss over my taking the carbine," he worried. Then Weisser was called down.

He also was down there a long time. He came back shaking his head and muttering pessimistically. Things had not looked at all good down there.

Lass went down next. He returned feeling a little better than Weisser. He thought we might get off with two or three years, he said brightly. "Naw-aw," said the irrepressible Harvey, "you won't get that much. You won't get more than six months. The British consul told me this was all mostly a matter of form!"

Then, Harvey went. Finally, "Clare!" resounded downstairs, and I went down.

It was a long, big room, that room downstairs. The Conseil sat at one end, before the windows. A row of officers, smartly uniformed, their medals on their breasts. A colonel sat in the center, then, flanking him on both sides, two majors, two captains and two lieutenants. I was taken to a chair and a little table to the right, where my counsel, the artillery captain, was already seated. Over to the left sat the prosecutor, a captain in the *Bataillon de Syrie*. He was a fat little man, and as I remembered the fat captain at Bosra, misgivings stirred me.

He rose, read the accusation, and I was taken before the Colonel of the Conseil de Guerre.

The colonel was a big, stout, heavy-faced man, with a little silver-gray clipped mustache, and cool blue eyes. He questioned me long, in a kindly way on the whole, bringing out my record. Now and then others along the bench questioned me. They seemed curious about my record in the World War, and brought out clearly the fact that I had fought in France with the Thirtieth Division. But still more curious they seemed as to the motive for my escapade. This, I sensed, would have a good deal to do in the measuring of my guilt. They questioned and questioned me on this—and I answered to the best of my knowledge—that I had been fed up with carrying big stones!

I went back to my place by my counsel, and then found I had friends. Rechad Bey was called in to testify. He was a red-headed Turk and had been my sergeant during the fighting at

Mousseifré. He made a wonderful witness for me, telling them how I had fought, that I had always obeyed officers and given the best I had. Then my counsel read a letter from Lieutenant Vernon.

The colonel halted him a moment. "You know," he said to me, "that your lieutenant has just died in Suweida?"

I did not know it. It seemed he had died of typhus there. I was affected at the news, but American fashion, I suppose, I showed little of it. All the eyes of the Conseil were on me. If only I had had a little Latin blood I could have helped myself there.

The letter was read. My lieutenant was dead, and here now, out of the tomb, he was speaking for me. I heard only snatches of phrases. "Clare was a *soldat remarquable*. . . He always did his duty, and more than his duty. . . He always obeyed orders. . . His coolness under fire was remarkable. . . In all his time of service, not one *punition*. . . Croix de guerre. . . His desertion incomprehensible. . . Probably due to a *coup de tête* which should not be too severely judged."

Thus from my dead lieutenant.

There were other letters. Even the corporal of my squad had written in.

I thought I was sitting pretty now. I was smiling within myself. I felt sure of a light sentence.

Then the prosecutor got up, and within a few sentences of the beginning of his peroration I knew that my misgivings over fat men had been correct.

Immediately, he placed my case squarely on the point most dangerous to me: whether I had simply deserted, or whether I had deserted "in the face of the enemy"—which might carry a sentence of death.

It was true, he admitted, that in the close environs of Suweida at the time of my desertion a limited peace reigned. But that was only a local condition. Fighting was still going on in other places; the war was still in progress; as the Conseil knew, it was still going on right here in Damascus itself.

It was true that my company had been at the time *en repos*, but that meant simply that it was in reserve, ready at any moment to take up arms again. The desertion of Gilbert Clare had been a desertion in the face of the enemy. The prosecutor thought he was doing only his duty in urging the Conseil to do theirs, by inflicting for this offense an exemplary punishment. And so on.

When he had finished I was given my chance. I was enraged and desperate. I had been studying the colonel and the members of the court-martial during this argument. I had seen the face of the colonel change, and the faces of the others change. I was desperate; the subtle danger and injustice in the fat man's argument had made me wild.

So I charged in with my bad and bastard but powerful Legion French. How could one call it war, I wanted to know, when you were in a place where men went for wood two kilometers from the post without their rifles? We had been at peace, in profound peace. Indeed this had been the very cause of my desertion; if we had been fighting I would have been there now. And we had been unjustly treated after long combats by being put to menial toil. I had enlisted in the Legion to fight, not to carry stones!

My counsel took the floor now, and after dwelling long on my record, tried to upset the prosecutor's thesis. He argued that troops *en repos* were not "in the face of the enemy."

The prosecutor answered, and soon the two

were in a battle royal, roaring at each other, almost throwing ink-wells. I was not altogether the only point at issue. My counsel, the artilleryman, was in active service; the other was a *rond de cuir*, a swivel-chair officer. The artilleryman could not hide his contempt, and the other his jealousy.

Finally, in a really impassioned burst, my counsel ended by again quoting my record, suggesting that my *malheureux coup de tête* be not taken too seriously. Throwing his client at the mercy of the court, he asked for a light sentence, with surcease.

And the Conseil rose, and the guard of honor presented arms, and the Conseil filed out, and I was marched back to our waiting-room upstairs.

We sat there, smoking cigarettes, very nervous, still discussing our chances. I was a bit worried. Weisser was sardonic. But Harvey had grown still more optimistic and thought by this time we'd get off with a few months. The gendarme at the door thought we'd get off lightly. Lass didn't know. Finally we persuaded ourselves we would not get much.

And then we were called down.

The Court had gone home. An adjutant read

the findings as we stood in line, the guard of honor—God knows why—at the "present arms."

First came Schop. His was a case of simple *promenade.* The adjutant read the preliminaries and then:

"Schop—five years at the *travaux forcés*!"

Lass gave me a quick look and his neck went red. Weisser chuckled diabolically. Harvey looked as if a mallet had just come down on his head.

Next came Weisser. "Weisser! Five years at the *travaux forcés*!"

"That's it, that's it," Weisser murmured sardonically. "Harvey said we were going to get a light sentence. That's a light sentence. Just five years!"

Lass followed. Also five years.

Then came Harvey. "Harvey! *Eight* years *aux travaux forcés*!"

Harvey's eyes were sticking out like those of a gored ox.

Then came little me. "Clare! Eight years *aux travaux forcés*!"

CHAPTER XVIII

EIGHT years in prison. At first we could not realize what that meant. A great anger had taken hold of us at what we felt was the unjust severity of the sentences, and all the way back in the black Maria, we raved and cursed and swore, without quite realizing what had happened to us.

But when I awoke the next morning! The sober contemplation of that! Eight years.

This meant eight years in confinement behind walls, in cells. The *travaux forcés*—hard labor—was a mere phrase, as the *travaux* had been abolished long ago. It meant eight years of strait confinement in military prisons.

There was still some hope, I found. That morning I wrote out an appeal from the sentence of the court.

Three days later it came back, *refusé*.

I was told there was another recourse, a last hope. I made out a demand for a surcease of the sentence.

Three days later it came back, *refusé*.

That was the end of the rope. And somehow or other, with this settled, I became calmer and tried to decide upon an attitude that might make these eight years and my coming through them sane, possible.

The consul was still coming to see me twice a week, each time having a hot meal brought in. He assured me that he had made his report to the State Department in such a way that the department would be interceding for me. I had got a cable from home; I was beginning to get letters from home, and was writing home.

On August 10, I was moved from Damascus to the prison in Beirut. I went alone, saying good-by to Harvey, Weisser and Lass, whom I thought I would never see again.

This prison was not bad as prisons go. It was immaculately clean, for one thing. Our bunks were sterile for a change, and we even had mosquito nets. The gendarme guards happened to be all good fellows, and the commandant just and kind. And I had been here only a few days when Harvey, Weisser and Lass arrived on another consignment. The prisoners were all military prisoners, or Arabs serving heavy sentences for rebellion.

At the end of two weeks, we were embarked on the transport *Jérusalem*, for Marseilles. Things continued to be not so bad. The quarters on board were not bad compared with what we had become used to as Legionaires. The ship crews treated us kindly, and lots of *ravio* food would be passed to us from the pantries. Still it was then that a sudden attack of despair and revolt took possession of us—probably at the thought of the long sentences which awaited us in France, which the ship so smoothly and inexorably was approaching. We longed for some great disaster. We saw ourselves in small boats, with a chance. Finally we actually got to the point where we tried to bring about our wild visionings. There was a loose hatch in which I kept dropping lit cigarettes in the hope of burning up the ship. The state of our desperation can be imagined from this. One day we almost succeeded. A fire started down there in the hold, but was promptly put out.

We arrived in Marseilles on September 1, were held in Fort St. Nicholas for two weeks, then were sent to the military prison of Albertville, in Savoie.

There we lost the last vestige of our military status. Our uniforms were taken away from us;

we put on shapeless dark-brown blouses and trousers and wooden shoes. Our heads were shaved, we were bertilloned, and recorded. And the long monotony which was supposed to be our lot for eight years began.

At that, things were still bearable. The food was not good, but it was not very bad, and the place was clean and free from vermin. It had been a monastery in old times, and we lived to the sound of the ancient bell that had once called the monks to their prayers. The bell routed us out at five-thirty; we had onion soup at six; at six-thirty we were taken upstairs to the work rooms.

This work was the making of uniforms for the army. They were given us partly made, and we finished them, sewing on the buttons and so on. I have never been able to handle a needle. In the Legion, I always had to ask Budney to sew on my buttons. We were supposed to finish three pairs of trousers a day—which I could never have done, were it not for a bit of luck which saved me from the accusations of insubordination, and the punishments which would surely have been mine.

The Corsican who sat next to me at the work

table had acquired a tailor's deftness with the needle. He could simply fly through the three pairs which were each man's share. On the other hand I was getting some money from home. So in return for cigarettes, razor blades, wine when I could get it, he saw to it that my three pairs of pants were completed every day.

This was a strictly military prison, and there were no real criminals here—though among some of those who had *refused* military service were Apaches and rather scummy gentlemen, together with a few real conscientious objectors and violent anarchists.

The modern week was in effect. We did not have to work on Saturday afternoons, nor Sundays, and we bathed every Saturday afternoon. We were allowed to write as many letters as we wanted, and were given free mailing twice a month to any place in France. I was writing continually to my mother and my father now. My father was assuring me that everything possible was being done, and that he had engaged a lawyer in Paris who was trying to obtain a change of sentence from the French Government. I was trying to train myself to patience, and every letter implored me to be submissive and warned me against any show of rebellion. Happily, here, the commandant, Captain Besançon, was a fine man. The outside guard, of Chasseurs Alpins, were also good fellows, as here, in this military prison, no taint of moral turpitude was attached to us.

Of course, it was prison all the same. And from our yard we could see the Alps, and the tall white-sheeted silhouette of Mt. Blanc!

Still, I was getting along fairly well. And on December 8 I received a bit of rare good news.

I was called down to the director's office. There an adjutant read an order apprising of the fact that my sentence had been commuted from eight years to four.

There is an immense difference between eight years of prison and four years of prison. I felt like celebrating. Instead I went quietly to dinner, and quietly to bed. But I knew that I had friends on the outside, and that they were tirelessly and successfully working for me.

What touched me was the way my fellow prisoners took the news—with unaffected gladness. "C'est chic, ça!" they said without any trace of envy, these poor fellows also in prison, but with no friends working for them outside and no hope of any shortening of their sentences.

And life went on, with its terrible monotony, but not so badly on the whole. I think I could have stood four years in Albertville and come out pretty well intact. But as Christmas day was nearing, a bit of bad news hit us all like a thunderbolt.

What had happened is an example of the way all human events are intertwined. France was at the time in the throes of a financial crisis. We were pressing it on the subject of its debts to us. The franc had been sliding down out of sight. Poincaré came into power with the intention of putting the finances in order.

His watchword was economy; he was enforcing it on all departments. And some genius discovered the fact that the military prisons were a costly luxury. Also an unnecessary one, since there existed prisons already, run much more cheaply, and built with perfectly good walls. In other words the civil prisons, where murderers, thieves, forgers, yeggs, the scum of France festered.

The military prisons were abolished; a law

was passed that military prisoners should serve their terms in the civil prisons.

This was the reason why, on Christmas day, Gilbert Clare and a few score of poor devils like him left Albertville where we had been, on the whole, moderately happy. It was a cold day of mud and sleet; we did not know just what it was all about, except that we were being transferred. Right at the station we began to have a taste of the nature of the change.

We expected to embark in a regular train. We found awaiting us the regular cellular compartments used in France for criminals. We had come already under the administration of our new masters.

Each cell was just wide enough for a man. It was not high enough to let him stand; he must sit all of the time on a little hard bench in a corner. Once the cell was closed—and closed they were—he was practically immobilized in that sitting position. Food and water were passed in to him through a little wicket in the door.

Thus we rode from Sunday morning to Monday morning, sitting upright motionless in the freezing cold.

When we got off we were at Clairvaux, in

Champagne, not far from the place where the A. E. F. headquarters had been during the War. We entered the main building of the prison of Clairvaux, an old monastery, seat of the famous Bernard de Clairvaux.

We were stiff and cold and sleepy and worried. Some of us—those of us who had any—had lit cigarettes. The roar of the Corsican guards ordered us to stamp them out, and right away we became acquainted with one of the most miserable hardships of our new régime. In Clairvaux prison, smoking was strictly forbidden, and any infraction of that rule severely punished.

We now received our new uniforms—a sort of double-breasted, short, collarless jacket of brownish homespun cloth, loose trousers of the same stuff, a sort of tam-o'-shanter (which, we found, we must always remove before a guard) and heavy wooden sabots. There were no socks. Your feet went bare into the hard wooden sabots.

We were marched into the refectory for breakfast. We sat on benches, with a higher bench in front, on which the food was placed. Here we got our second or third lesson as to what awaited us. The guards savagely commanded silence. We were not allowed to speak in the refectory. Nor, we discovered later, in the cell. To the dreary discomfort of not being allowed to smoke, in this prison was added the still more dreary one of almost perpetual silence.

The director addressed us, and told us of the rules to which we would be restrained. Although the prison was surrounded with shops in which the convicts made wooden shoes, nails, wire and clothing, there was not enough of such work for us new-comers; there would be no work for us.

We would receive food twice a day, meat on Thursdays and Sundays. Smoking was prohibited. Also talking in the cell house and the refectories. It was allowed in the yard.

Any infraction of the rules would be pitilessly punished, with the bread-and-water punishment, the cachot (solitary cell), or the *salle de discipline*, about which we would find out later.

By the next day, we had been swung fully into the routine of our new existence.

We got up at seven, cleaned our cells, and filed down to the dining-room. There we got a *boule* of black prison bread, which seemed to me to be made of sawdust. The prison furnished no coffee, but you could buy it if you had money.

We were kept in the dining-room an hour, and then our first section was sent out into the yard for exercise. This division into sections was necessary because there was not enough room in the yard for every one. So one half of us went out while the other half remained in the refectory. Throughout the day we were to alternate thus, each section out for an hour, in for another, out again for another hour.

The first half hour of every hour outside was spent marching in file, in a dead silence, around and around in a circle following the walls of the yard. In the center of the circle stood a guard, calling out, "right, left, right, left," giving us our marching step to which we must rigidly keep time. When this had been done for a half hour, we were ordered to sit on stone benches that went around the yard. We were all numbered, and wore the numbers on white brassards around our left arms. And we had to sit ever according to our numbers. So, although for this short half hour we were allowed to speak, we could talk only to the men whom the numbering had put close, and not to the friends we might have chosen. In all the time I was in Clairvaux I never sat—my number was twelve, and theirs far from it—near Harvey, Weisser or Lass. My nearest neighbors were Bouet, a Frenchman in for five years for striking a sergeant, Catron, another who had insulted a captain, and Davin, who was serving five years because he had grabbed a corporal by the shoulders and had shaken him. These men were all from regular metropolitan regiments, Frenchmen *called to the colors*. But there were many also from the colonial troops—Algerians, Tunisians, Moroccans, Syrians. And some had been thieves and a few murderers. We were kept apart, however, from the civil prisoners in other buildings of the prison.

That first hour period outside was partly taken up in washing. There was within the building no wash-stand of any kind. But in the court was a hydrant. At this lone hydrant we washed, in squads of four or five, with others pressing behind, with just time enough to dash a little water into our faces and quickly brush our teeth—if we brushed them—which I did as a part of the saving self-discipline I had put myself to. We were having a severe winter; it was freezingly cold out there, and with feet bare in the wooden shoes, weak with the insufficient food, we nearly died while washing or waiting for our turn to wash.

All the rest of the day, each section would go out for an hour, march silently in file for the half of that, and sit motionless on the benches for the second half. After that it would go inside while the other section did the same. Then out it would go again.

Shortly after ten o'clock we had our first real meal of the day. This consisted of a soup which was hardly more than warm water with a little bread in it, and a ration of eight teaspoonfuls of either beans, lentils, or peas. On Thursdays and Saturdays a little piece of meat, half the size of one's hand, was added—tough, stringy meat, like leather.

At five-twenty we had a similar meal, and half an hour later were marched to the cell room. There we were lined up, searched, locked up—and then to bed. There was no heat, we were glad to get into our bunks.

The cell room, as a matter of fact, was a sort of house of refuge to me. The bunks were good, the blankets sufficient. Though the cells were very small, this did not matter much since they were used only at night. On the contrary, by going to sleep as soon as possible, one could steal out of the time of one's deadly sentence a full twelve hours every night, since the awakening was at seven. Twelve hours every night in forgetfulness of our misery; I made the most of it.

In the cell house silence reigned as it did in the refectories. The cells—just large enough for the cot and for one to stand beside it—were of reinforced concrete on three sides while the fourth side was of close wire meshing, as was the ceiling. For each section of thirty men there was a *prévôt*, a sort of trustee with disciplinary powers. An electric button was in his cell. If any one talked, he pressed the button and the guard came up from his post downstairs. The *prévôt* said nothing to him. But the guard went along the rows calling out in turn the names of the men in each cell. As he passed the guilty one, the *prévôt* silently nodded his head, and the guard knew, although we had not heard the *prévôt* speak a word.

The culprit would then be ordered to report to the director in the *prétoire* in the morning. The director was a big Marseillais, not an unkind man, but he was used to handling the real criminals of civilian prisons and seemed unable to make any difference when it came to us. He had an assistant, a black-bearded man with shaven upper lip whom we all cordially hated and called *le bouc*—the he-goat—who was really brutal and cruel. The director's *prétoire* was fixed up with all the apparatus of a court room. There was a bar behind which he sat, and opposite which the accused stood. The accusation would be made in writing and read by the *greffier*, or clerk. What justice there was resided entirely in the apparatus. The accused had no one to defend him. The *greffier* would ask him, "Have you anything to say?" and it was always better to say nothing. Your word counted for nothing, the guard's for everything, and the latter got even with you for what you had said—if you had said anything—by beating you up in the cachot later.

Then to the man who had talked in the cell room—or committed any other infraction of the savagely severe rules—would come the sentence. It would be "four days on bread and water," or "eight days on bread and water." Or it might be the *salle de discipline* or it might be the cachot.

We called the punishment of the *salle de discipline* the "espadrille." In the *salle de disci-*

pline you were set to marching around and around the room all day, doing as much as forty kilometers between morning and night in that confined space. But there was another trick to it. To do this marching, you took off your wooden sabots and put on *espadrilles*. These were sandals with soles made of twisted rope. The rope soon cut into your feet, and you went on around and around on feet that burned and bled.

The cachot was the equivalent of the dungeon cell of American prisons. In this old abbey, the cachots were down deep in the bowels of the earth. Yet men would be sentenced to as much as sixty days in them—which meant they left them only for the hospital.

All this was aggravated by the brutality of the Corsican guards. They had unlimited power; you doffed your cap when you stood before one. You were supposed to stand their worst insults silently, without answering. And the sense of their prestige was easily hurt in them, and they avenged themselves by passing *au tabac* the punished man; that is, in the cachots, or the *salle de discipline*, anywhere they were alone with him, out of sight of witnesses, they ganged him and mercilessly beat him up.

Under the admonitions which continually came to me in letters from home and also from the consulate, I had made up my mind to stand everything without a murmur rather than jeopardize the efforts being made for me on the outside. "Even if a guard kicks me I'll take it without saying anything," I kept saying to myself, trying to be ready in case any such moment came.

I could see little of my comrades of the unfortunate "promenade" over the hill. Weisser seemed to be getting along better than any of us, what with his sardonic sense of humor and his philosophy which did not expect much better out of life. He had got a job in the cleaning squad which policed, served out the soup, and so forth—and that was better than the enforced idleness which made our days so desperately long. Harvey and Lass had had a quarrel and finally had come to blows in the court as both were washing at the hydrant one morning—for which they had got three days in the cachot each.

I could see Harvey a few moments each day in this way. My cell was at the end of the long corridor and was one of the last locked when we were shut in for the night. As the guard went down the line locking each cell in turn, the prisoner standing inside meekly at attention the while, cap in hand, I would have time to loiter a minute or two against the wire meshing of Harvey's cell, and exchange a bit of small talk.

I was training myself to unlimited patience; I was determined to do nothing to jeopardize any chance I might have at all of getting out of this hell. And thus came to a painful moment where I had to make a painful decision.

CHAPTER XIX

BENEATH the wretched life in Clairvaux, the iron discipline, the long periods of silence, the deadly monotony and hopelessness, a fire always smoldered, flaring out suddenly now and then.

On the very day after our arrival from Albertville, there had been a fight. Cold, hungry, nerves raw with the deprivation of tobacco, we of the new draft were in the corridor of the cell room, about to be searched and locked up as we were every night, when an Algerian, who had been in the Spahis, got into an argument with a French soldier.

The Frenchman finally struck the Algerian. Another Algerian sprang to the aid of his fellow countryman, which brought another Frenchman into the fight in his turn. This continued till the corridor was a welter of forty or fifty men fighting with everything they had. At first it was fists and heels; then they took off the heavy wooden sabots they wore and smashed away with these. Then some got heavy billets of stove wood. The guards, storming in with their riding crops, added to the confusion; bedlam reigned. So wild was the mêlée that for a long time the guards seemed unable to stop it. Skulls were being cracked and eyes gouged out. When the guards finally succeeded, several men were staggering about badly hurt and an Algerian was lying in a pool of blood on the concrete floor.

Dozens of men were taken to the cachots after that. The rest of us were lined up in the court to hear a speech from the director so full of threats as to what could and would be done to us that it left us thoroughly cowed.

But a few months later came another affair.

My section was in the yard, and for some reason or other we were not marching that day. And some of the lighter-hearted prisoners began to play leap-frog like small boys at school. They got to laughing and shouting; their play filled the usually silent yard with noise.

The window of the head guard's office opened on the court. The shouts of the game annoyed him and several times he ordered quiet. The men would play the game quietly for a while, then forget and shout again. Finally a guard ordered us to our benches—the stone benches that went around the yard and on which we sat in numerical order.

In childish defiance, then, a little bit of a Frenchman started to sing, and soon many of the others joined in. The guard ordered silence, but the men continued to sing. The guard threatened to call the head guard, and still they went on singing.

There were among those on the bench two whom every one liked. They were Parisians, one nicknamed "Le Boeuf," the other "Bamboule." They were both young, full of Parisian *blague*, played the clown together, and were an amusement to us in our black life.

After a while the guards picked on the little fellow who had started the singing and started to drag him off. But the men to the right and left of him held on to him and would not let him go. The chief of the guards was called, but still the men around the little fellow held him and kept him from being dragged to the cachot, where he was undoubtedly bound. Their defiance was still half playful, but the yard was getting into an uproar of excitement.

Finally the guard blew his whistle and the director of the prison came running out of his office. He came up, and immediately selected Bamboule out of the whole crowd. "Come with me, Bamboule," he said.

But Bamboule would not go. "What do you want with me?" he asked. "Why should I go? I haven't done anything." It was a fact that he had taken no part in what had been going on.

"Come with me, Bamboule," said the director again.

"To be beaten up in the cachot by the guards?" said Bamboule. "Not much. I won't go."

"I give you my word of honor you will not be beaten," said the director. "But you must come with me."

But the director's word of honor did not mean much to Bamboule, and he still refused to go.

The guards then charged at Bamboule. He put his back against the wall, took off a sabot, and holding it threateningly, dared them to come on. Then his friend Le Boeuf took his position against the wall next to Bamboule and drew off his sabot.

A guard approached Bamboule. Down came his wooden shoe on the guard's head. And down came Le Boeuf's on another guard's head. An uproar followed, a free-for-all fight, and finally Bamboule and Le Boeuf were dragged off by the infuriated guards who were cuffing and kicking them toward the long corridors that led to the cachots.

That night at dinner, no one ate. This was not an arranged strike, but our nerves were so taut at the violence and injustice perpetrated, and at this new evidence of the hopelessness of our lot, that we could not eat. We were all, down to the lowest character of us, literally too sick to eat.

I had taken no part in any of what had happened, remembering the constant counsel I got from the outside. But I also could not eat.

The next morning, when we came down from the cell room for our *boule* of bread, each of the refectories was locked up as soon as its section was within.

Then one was opened and that section marched into the yard.

When it came to the turn of my section, I found out what was being done.

In the court forty guards were massed, all armed with loaded carbines.

We were halted and the director went slowly

down the line. To each man as he came to him, he asked just one question. "*Vous mangez?*" "Are you eating?"

If the man said "yes," he remained in the line.

If he said "no," he was dragged away by the guards. They threw themselves on him; they dragged him to the long corridor that led to the cachots. As they dragged him to the corridor, we saw them kicking and cuffing him. As he went along the black corridor out of our sight, we could hear his curses and his shrieks, and the dull sound of the carbine butts pounding his body.

When the director reached me a sudden impulse of violent revolt nearly doomed me. But I mastered myself. I had taken no part in the game of leap-frog, in the singing, in the resultant fighting. This was none of my affair. And my sympathy for the men being punished, my hatred of the whole régime, I smothered in the memory of the words I constantly got from home beseeching me to be careful, be careful, to be patient and bear everything. When the director came to me and said, "Do you eat?" I answered, "I eat."

I sank after that into a pretty deep abyss. Though letters still came from home, assuring me that efforts were going on in my behalf, I could hardly believe I could get out of this inferno.

The rules had been made still more severe after the last outbreak. All those who had said they would not eat were placed in the "special quarter" in bare cells with no bed or blanket, where they slept on the cold floor. And those gay monkeys, Le Boeuf and Bamboule, were given each eighty days in the cachot—an almost incredible sentence.

As for the rest of us, our lot was made harder. Our rations of food were cut down. What they called our "privileges" were curtailed. We were never allowed to stand in the yard now; we must march around and around, or sit in numerical order on the stone benches. The privilege of an "extra" letter was taken away. You were regularly allowed once a month to write two letters, and the privilege we had been granted was the permission to write each month another letter, called *lettre spéciale*, which meant a letter to some official—the consul in my case—from which the writer expected perhaps help or a change of sentence. This *lettre spéciale*—the last and only guard most of the prisoners had against complete despotism—was now forbidden. The privilege of talking to the director once a week was taken away, which placed us altogether at the mercy of the sub-directors and the guards. The entire attitude hardened. And those of the guards who had been lenient now became as hard-boiled as the worst of the others.

I fell into an obsession, brooding upon the special injustice being done us. We had committed no crime which is recognized as a civil crime, yet we were being treated like civil criminals—as though we had murdered, stolen, or raped. This kept turning and turning in my head. Why should we be treated as criminals, we who were simply military offenders?

What helped to save me were the books. There was a small library in the prison, and during the hours in the *réfectoire* when we had to sit silent on our crowded benches, we were allowed to read. The prison library afforded a rather childish fare, but there on my bench in the refectory, I went through "Twenty Thousand Leagues Under the Sea" and every other book of Jules Verne, and every book of Mayne Reid, traveling with those authors all over the earth, and away from the earth. They were in French of course, but by this time I knew enough of the language to make out most of the stuff, and to guess at what I couldn't make out. Whenever too badly stuck, I braved *punition* and asked some Frenchman to help me out. And finally came a package from home, in which I found books for which I had asked—a history of England and a geography of the United States!

I wrote home a good deal, as here I was more lucky than the French prisoners. Their mail was examined, and so little of it got by that it discouraged them from writing. But some one in that office was evidently too lazy to have my letters translated. Everything seemed to go through and I wrote more and more freely.

Still it was a pretty low and discouraged Gilbert Clare who, coming down in line from the cell house, one September morning, had his sleeve plucked by a guard.

I had been noticing this guard for a moment as we filed down into the refectory. He was rudely catching each man by the arm as he passed, to read the number on his brassard. I came along, and now he caught at my arm and twisted it around to read the number on my white brassard. "Numéro douze?" he asked.

That was my number. Twelve. I came to attention, holding my cap in my hand.

"Your name is Clare?"

"Yes."

He looked at the paper he had in his hand. "But you have another name, too?"

"Doty," I said.

"Ah, *c'est ça*," he said, satisfied. "Come with me."

But I was the reverse of satisfied. What did this sinister break in the routine mean? What had I done? I racked my memory trying to remember what breach of what rule I might have been guilty of. He turned me over to another guard, who took me to the *Quartier*—where the punishment cells were. "What have you done now?" this one growled as we went along. "*Rien*," I said, "I've done nothing at all." "But you must have," he insisted. "*C'est malheureux, quand même*—you're going to be punished again—don't you know how to behave yourself?"

I was getting more and more uneasy. What had I done to call punishment down upon me? I couldn't think of anything.

He placed me in a cell, and the next step puzzled me still more. He took away my prison uniform, and gave me another to put on, an old one, almost worn out. Then he locked the cell.

My wonder increased as I examined the cell. It was a rather large cell, lined with wood; it wasn't a bad cell at all. And there was no bunk in it!

I remained locked there an hour, pacing to and fro, nervous as a witch and worried. Then a *prévôt* brought me from the kitchens the cup of coffee I had ordered for breakfast and pushed it in through the wicket. He was a kindly fellow. Keeping his face in the small opening a moment, he tried to reassure me. "*C'est rien*," he said. "It is nothing. You'll see. There are no charges against you."

This time, after drinking the coffee, I sat down with my back to the wall. Although I was not certain the *prévôt* was right, I felt a little better.

I remained in the cell maybe another hour, and then another guard put his face to the wicket. "You are going to be turned out," he said.

"No!" I said. "Why do you tell me such stuff as that?"

"It's true," he insisted. "You have been *gracié*—you have been pardoned."

I now began to go up and down the cell like a madman. Now and then I'd break into an actual run, unable to hold down my excitement. What was it that was happening? Was this old guard right? Or was he cruelly kidding me?

Another half hour, and I was called out and presented with a bundle—and recognized the military uniform in which I had come here, and all my personal effects. My heart began to race still faster within me.

They left me there in a little court for about twenty minutes. Then I was called into the *prétoire*. And it was true!

The director read it. I caught only phrases—but they were enough! "By the order of the President of the Republic!" "*Rémission totale* of sentence!" Oh, yes, those two phrases were enough; I did not listen to much of the rest. I was once more a Legionaire. I was no longer a convict.

The *prétoire* was holding court. It was full of poor devils come for sentence. And the director did not miss his chance. He made them a speech. Quite an eloquent little speech. In which he held me up to them, both me and what had happened to me, as an example and a lesson. I had obeyed all the rules—and lo—see?—now I was free!

Then the director, seemingly sympathetic of my good luck, shook me by the hand, and bade me *au revoir* (but I had no intention of ever seeing him again) and *bonne chance.*

There were papers to sign—in France there are always papers to sign; I was given two letters from home which had arrived that very morning, and the seven hundred and seventy francs that remained of my money, and an order for transportation which was good as far as Troyes—from where I was to keep on going to Marseilles, to report there at the Dépôt of the Legion. Then I took off my prison clothes and put on my good old uniform!

A clerk kept bothering me during the whole of this operation. He kept telling me to hurry up, that my train was leaving at twelve. My train was leaving at twelve! I loafed a bit on purpose just to hear him repeating that phrase. My train was leaving at twelve!

Then a guard took me to the gate; the guard at the gate let me through; and I was alone and free.

The first thing I did when I had gone a few

steps was to open my bundle, kneel down to it and extract from it my old pipe and a package of Maryland tobacco which had been taken away from me on my coming. I filled the pipe, lit it and took a last look at the Maison Rouge—the Red House—as we had come to call the sinister prison. I had been there nine months. Sixteen months had gone by since, down there on the Syrian-Transjordanian frontier, I had raised my hands to the Syrian gendarme's shot.

Swinging my bundle, puffing my pipe, I sauntered down to the little station, and got my ticket. The train—my train!—just a little way down the track, was coming in with a roar.

CHAPTER XX

WELL, all the rest of it is down hill. I left Clairvaux at twelve and was in Troyes at three. The train for Dijon did not leave before seven; my stay in Troyes has remained memorable to me chiefly on account of the remarkable meal to which I treated myself in the station restaurant, the best restaurant I ever came across in the whole world! From Dijon to Lyons and from Lyons to Marseilles, I was on a train so full that I had to stand up all the way in the aisle. But I stood up in the aisle and didn't grumble at all!

It was morning when I reached Marseilles and reported at the Legion dépôt, Fort St. Jean. The sergeant in the office looked at me goggle-eyed. "Clare, *nom de Dieu*, how did you get here?" I told him I had been *gracié*, and I got congratulations all around. And just a little later I saw a squat little red-haired fellow in the court, and went to him, and turned him around—and it was Rechad Bey, my old sergeant of the Mousseifré fight, he who had so valiantly testified for me at the court-martial. We went and made a *tour* at the canteen, and I felt I was home once more.

He was leaving that very day for Bel Abbes, but I could not go with him. I followed a few days later, however, in charge of about forty *bleus*.

It was the same trip I had made two years before—a hundred years ago. Then I was a recruit, and penniless. Now I was in charge of recruits; I was a veteran, to say the least, in more ways than one. And I had money, lots of money in my pocket; and something had happened to me which made everything seem delectable. What a nice trip that was!

Finally, I was marching my *bleus* up through the back ways (just as once I had been marched) into Bel Abbes. And there, at the gates of the Legion *caserne* stood waiting to greet me not only Rechad Bey but Sergeant d'Etienne, who after a year's civilian life had rejoined the Legion! What a pleasing reunion we had at the canteen!

Then the old garrison life I had not forgotten. I was in Compagnie de Passage Numéro 2—the same sort of outfit as that in which I had been just before leaving for Syria. The captain greeted me Legion fashion with a long bawling out expressing his hope that I would now behave. That was like old times, I grinned inside of me.

The Vingt-neuvième was still in Syria. The citadel seemingly had been finished, and they were in peace quarters in the north. From Bel Abbes every day, almost, heavy drafts were leaving for the fighting in Morocco. I asked to go and was given the old familiar answer, "You'll go when you are called, no sooner, no later." And then, "But you'll be called all right, all right!"

And then it was the old garrison life. Making your bed, sweeping, swabbing. Arranging the *paquetage* in its mathematical symmetry, with not a thread sticking out. Chamber inspections to see that the blankets and the sheets were placed exactly right on the bed, that your shoes were in the precisely correct spot, that nothing stuck out of the *paquetage*, that there was no dust on the shelf where the *paquetage* reposed, and no dust under the bed, that the *bidon* was empty as fixed by regulations, and hanging upside down with stopper out. And guard duty, and drills. And dress inspections—and washings and furbishings and shining of buttons and polishing of shoes. Most of your time off was supposed to be given to washing clothes. And the different *corvées*—the

peeling of potatoes and cutting up of carrots. I heard others grumble around me: I laughed at them. Between five and nine—if not on guard duty—you were free; and the town offered amusing and colorful distractions, Caucasian and Oriental, and the canteens were hospitable to a veteran with money in his pocket. In the Legion no one cares how much a man drinks as long as he does not get drunk. And that term is elastic in the Legion. You are not drunk as long as you molest no one, and are able to get up the stairs to your bed *à quatre pattes*—on all fours.

Thus October passed, and November. There was much rain and cold; you stood guard often in a perpendicular rain. Then at the end of November, my name was on the list of a new draft going to Mekinez, in Morocco, to join there the Second Regiment of the Legion. I was to be off again, thank God.

I drew a new uniform, new equipment; I had my hair clipped again; I went the rounds saying good-by. I found I was to travel as far as Fez with Thompson, an American from New York state, an ex-gob who had already served five years in the Legion, had reënlisted and whose regiment was at Marrakech while mine was in Mekinez.

But before leaving for Morocco there was to be a review as a send-off to us. In fact there were to be two reviews. One of the company by the captain, in the morning; and a big one of the whole garrison by the colonel in the afternoon.

So we were all up early, cleaning, rubbing, furbishing, the "*sous-offs*" as officious as wet-nurses. The first review was to be at nine. Just a little before that time came a runner from the colonel's office ordering me to report there at nine.

As the company review was at nine, and I could not be in two places at the same time, I took my troubles to the *adjudant-chef*, who judiciously decided the colonel's order held precedence, and excused me from the parade.

So I went to the colonel's office, and as my comrades were being reviewed, stood before the colonel's aide.

"Gilbert Clare," he called.

"Present!" I answered, coming to attention.

He had a telegram in his hand. He looked at it, made as if to read, then stopped. "Do you understand French?" he asked.

"Oui, mon capitaine," I answered, beginning to get very much excited.

He took up the telegram again, and this time

read it. And I understood enough French to know what it said.

By orders of the President of the Republic and the Minister of War, I was *libéré*—free of my enlistment in the Legion—mustered out—free!

I came out of there in a daze. The rest was a good deal of a daze. I signed papers, I turned in my uniform and equipment and was given the strange garments with which the Legion bids good-by to its own. I went around bidding farewells, with every one wishing me *bonne chance.* I went to see Colonel Rollet.

He looked at me just a bit sardonically with those terrible blue eyes of his. He did not tell me exactly that I should have been shot, but he kept repeating, "Gilbert Clare, *vous avez de la chance. Vous avez de la chance.* You are a lucky boy."

Then he said, "I know you will write about the Legion. Try to tell the truth. It is true we are hard. But we are just. *Nous sommes durs, mais justes.*"

Then he shook my hand and bade me *au revoir* and *bonne chance.*

I went out through the big gates, with my bundle, in my funny clothes. And at the gates I stopped a moment. And what should come along at this moment but the *Clique*. There they came, bass drum beating, drums rolling, fifes shrieking, the bugles and trumpet screaming, playing the old march I knew so well—"Louis Quatorze."

I turned back to the fort and said, "To hell with you!"

But that was simply because, unreasonably enough—here I was on the way back to the United States!—to that stirring, screaming music, to that fast, fast gay beat, I had felt my spine begin to rise and a tear come to my eye.

I broke away and started off toward the dock where the little tub transport *Tafna* was tied up ready to cross over to Marseilles.